# The YEAR THAT AGED US

2020 poetry collection

by **Eric Nixon**

Cover design by Eric Nixon.



ISBN: 978-0-9984362-6-5

BISAC: Poetry / American / General



That being said, I'm pretty flexible with fully credited adaptations. Please contact me if you are considering adapting or remixing any works contained within this book.

All situations depicted in this book are products of the author's imagination and may not match any reality known to otherwise exist elsewhere.

"From Here To There" was previously published on the Epic Group Writers website as the winning poem for the June 2020 writing contest.

Published by Double Yolk Press in Edmonds, Washington.

EricNixonAuthor@gmail.com

EricNixon.net

# AUTHOR'S FOREWARD

There are a lot of words that could be used to describe 2020, although not *all* of them are terrible. Despite the bad stuff, this year was pretty big for me. We moved from the Amherst/Northampton area of western Massachusetts to beautiful Edmonds, Washington. I resumed my career as a hotel manager. I wrote and published *You Are A Poet*, a guided poetry book, with Kari Chapin. I joined the Epic Group Writers in Edmonds, and won a writing contest. I also wrote this book you are holding in your hands, which is, by far, my largest poetry collection.

This book is meant to be my poetic diary for the year. It's where I let my creativity go crazy being inspired by everything from COVID-19, to politics, to nature, to spirituality. All of my observances distilled into poems are here. That's really the main job of a poet – to observe and report.

This collection contains all 320 poems I wrote over the year. I guess that means there was a lot to report on in 2020.

Thank you for spending this time with me. I greatly appreciate it.

Enjoy!

Eric

# TABLE OF CONTENTS

A Bankable Given
A Release
Foil To The Land
Hate Corner
Aggressively Orange
From Here To There
Tilt
Is The Same As The Gray

**July** – 12 poems
Super Slouching
Plain And Boring
The Year That Aged Us
Repeated Exposure To Joy
There Is A Reverence With The Process
The Captain Of The Boat
Give Whales Space
Watching The News
Inspired By The Movement
Generations Removed
I've Gone Over My Time Limit
Get Some Water In Your Eyes

**August** – 30 poems
Dandelions
Laundromat
More Is A Mindset Beyond
Evolutionary Point
Focus On The Speck
Choosing To Grow
Truly Terrifying
Noticed The Southern Movement
Seeing The Smooth Orange Tinting
The Tattered Scraps Of Your Present Self
Bringing The Universe Closer
The Rhythm Of Life
Up Early For A Saturday

**September** – 50 poems

Steering Me Right
Impact
Particulates
Overshadowed
Stepping Out
Point Of View
The Color Above
Willing To Break It Completely
American Re-Revolution
The Gentle Pitter Patter
Preordained
Is There A Ghost
Building This Thing
Into The Skip-Beat
A Greater Whole
Not Ready To Waive
The Ones That Missed
Not Blind
Reviewing A Checklist
Obligation Is The Road
Brevity
Interruption
The Pervasive Chill
West Coasting
Like Bokeh In My Body
Freedom To Be A Jumble
Society Has Devolved
Left For The Day
More Pictures

**October** – 55 poems
Shedding Skin
Unsurprising
The Heap Of Thoughts
Muting The Moon
Quantum Entanglement
Distillation
Go With The Flow

Reaching Out
The Invisible Killer
The Summer I Misplaced
The Universe Is Guiding
Forward Is The Only Direction
Unproven
Pinballing Through Life
Complexing The Identity
Like Watching Old Episodes

**November** – 52 poems
Waiting Is The Hardest Part
The Cliffhanger Conclusion
Submerged
Nightlight Of Hope
Completely Unaware
Pushed Past Normalcy
A Lingering Flash
Each And Every Day
The Remaining Leaves
Onward To Adventure
Bonsai
Dropping It All
The Shiny Objective
Forgotten
Favorite Thing
Relentless Momentum
Digging Deeply
Opinion Hosts
Embellishment
The Past Is A Lively Cat
A Toleration
Early Christmas
Standing In The Shadow
A Life Delineated By Topography
Smug Suits
Long Light Reaching
Blizzard Of Anvils

A Cute Fuzzybutt
The Bulking Time Of The Year
A Landscape Changed
A Much-Deserved Break

**2020 total: 320**

# JANUARY

**The Next Moment**

January 1st – here we are
The promise of a new month
The beginning of a new year
At the start of a new decade
And I feel like I need to be
Careful as to set the tone right
For all of this newness
Like seeing fresh snow
Just covering the yard
Free from any footprints
Knowing I'm going to be
The first to step across it
That's how this moment
Right here, right now, feels
When I know I should just
Disregard the sentiment
And get going, start running
Setting the pace for the year
And this confliction is causing
Me to pause…just slightly
Where it might actually
Trip me up, make me fall
Which, when I get going
I don't want to look back and see
The floundering marks
Of the undecided me
I would rather know
That I just went all-out
Confidently in a direction –
But to know, and to do
Are two different things
And the next moment
Is the one that decides
How all of this starts

January 1, 2020
Whately, Massachusetts

**Title Goes Here**

Starting the year
By writing poetry
As I normally do
I open my template
For my poetry books
But I need a name
Anything at all
Just as a placeholder
So, I come up with
Something catchy:
*Title Goes Here*

January 1, 2020
Whately, Massachusetts

I don't know how I'll feel about myself if I don't end up changing it and I actually name this collection, *Title Goes Here*. There's a 50% chance I'll be disappointed in myself for not coming up with something more interesting, and another 50% where I like it for the carefree nature of it. Let's see what I do in a year from now.

Update: It's a year later (January 2, 2021) and I am glad I did not name this collection *Title Goes Here*.

**The Folly Of Winter**

The folly of winter where
The worker finished shoveling
Just a few minutes ago
And moved on somewhere else
When the rumble came
And the avalanche of snow
Cascaded off the roof
Buying the sidewalk
He spent so long clearing
And then, a short time later
His boss stopped by
And got mad at the worker
Thinking he didn't do his job

January 1, 2020
Whately, Massachusetts

True story!

**Sandwiched In By The Work Week**

Today is the first day of the year
It doesn't seem like it though
I think because it's a Wednesday.
Big events like this are better saved
For the weekend when
It can be better appreciated
Instead of glossed over
Sandwiched in by the work week
Lessening the impact
This day deserves

January 1, 2020
Whately, Massachusetts

It's been tough remembering to type "2020" instead of "2019." I'm 1 for 4 so far this year.

**Softening To Soot**

What little light is out there
Right now at five o'clock
Is the kind of duskiness
Where the sky looks like
A uniformly light ash
Gently softening to soot
And will, undoubtedly soon,
Cover absolutely everything

January 13, 2020
Whately, Massachusetts

## A Tender Punch

People often say
That the Universe
Often gives them
A kick in the ass
In order to get them
Up, and moving along
But, to me, that sounds
A little rough and
Unnecessarily tough
When in actuality
What it gives you
Is a lot more like
A tender punch –
Just enough
To wake you up
To let you know
You've got to
Get going on your stuff
Sometimes it hurts
Just a little
But nothing like
What'd happen
If you kept napping
Or dawdling at life

January 18, 2020
Whately, Massachusetts

**Snowman On A Diet**

With the warming winter
The newfound heat
Ends up putting every
Snowman on a diet
Thinning the mass
Slimming the curves
Melting away the pounds
Affecting their ability
To pose, to stand,
And to just exist
Because a puddle
With sticks and a hat
Is harder to build
And a lot less fun

January 25, 2020
Whately, Massachusetts

# FEBRUARY

**Hold The Moment**

Standing on the back steps
While the dog does his thing
Looking out over the back yard
Which has been my view for years
Trying to hold the moment
For as long as I possibly can
Knowing that in two weeks
Everything will radically change
And I won't see my daily life
From this perspective again

February 7, 2020
Whately, Massachusetts

We are going to be moving to the Seattle area. It's weird to think that the life you've known for a couple of years, the daily everything you've been used to can suddenly, radically change to something so completely unknown, and what you used to know is something you'll never see again.

**The Last Day Of Work**

The last day of work
Going through emails
Clearing out my inbox,
Things that were once
SO IMPORTANT
Are now…well, not so much
And are deleted with ease,
Full of things I always meant to do
Apart from the bare walls
Where my photos once were
And the empty inbox
It doesn't seem real
That I'll never in my life
Be back here
Where I've come
Every weekday for years
And my immediate plans
Are so many miles away
It doesn't seem real
Until the moment
I walk out the door
So, I make it a point
To be hyper-aware of "lasts"
Such as the last time
I'll do this,
See that,
Or talk to someone
And while in each "last"
I make a conscious effort
To preserve the moment
To remember the mundane
To savor the feel
To make sure I remember
What this place was like
So someday
In case I want to recall
What it was like here

In this placeholder of a job
In this in-between point in my life
I can experience every detail
Vividly, like a movie

February 12, 2020
Northampton, Massachusetts

My last day in the Fiscal office at the VA Medical Center in Northampton.

# MARCH

**This New Place**

Despite the ongoing
And rapidly growing plague
Spreading all around me
I am really enjoying
This new place I'm living
The views, the experiences,
The new life I'm building
In this place between
The sea and the mountains
Like nowhere I've been before

March 8, 2020
Everett, Washington

Note: reading this a year later, it's interesting to see my first mention of COVID-19. Basically, the area we moved to was where the first cases and deaths were from the virus, so that was pretty scary.

**Reminders Of Back There**

I've noticed that I seem to be
Surrounded with the things,
The reminders of home,
Well, let me re-phrase that –
Reminders of back there
The place I left
The place I chose to walk away from
In favor of my new home
But the past is a clingy thing
So, the reminders will continue
And that's okay because
I'm confident in my decision
To change the location of my life
To something better-resonating
With how I want to be

March 8, 2020
Everett, Washington

## Inspired By A Cross-Country Trip

I've always been intrigued
With creatives who are inspired
By a cross-country trip
And are able to write a book,
Make an album, or something similar
Now that I've done the trip
Several times myself
I've found that the only
Inspiration I have
Is to avoid doing it
And instead, choose to fly

March 8, 2020
Everett, Washington

I was specifically thinking of Tori Amos's album, *Scarlet's Walk.* Personally, I think driving cross-country is a terrible slog (especially in winter).

**Take Advantage Of The Offerings**

The opportunities to explore
In a new-to-you location
Are seemingly endless
The thing is to actually
Take advantage of the offerings
So, if you ever leave
You don't leave with regrets

March 8, 2020
Everett, Washington

Note: it's a year later and I still have not been able to explore or see anything in the area because of the virus.

**The Sentence Formed By The Symphony**

At the café
Writing
Wishing
I had remembered
My headphones
To block out the sounds
Of the clanging
The clinking
The running of the washer
The beeping of the microwave
The forgettable music
Lightly on in the background
The whooshing of the coffee maker
The droning murmur
Of the conversation
Rising from the other tables
Interspersed with laughs
The soft slamming
Of the front door
Punctuating the sentence
Formed by the symphony of sounds
Found in this average café
On this normal Sunday

March 8, 2020
Everett, Washington

I'm at the Shut Up & Write Meetup at The Loft Coffee Bar. When I first got here, I realized I had forgotten my headphones, but it turns out that I don't actually miss them.

**Some Things Change**

Some things change
Sometimes the wrong things
But in the end
We realize they were
The right things
Because we couldn't imagine
A present any other way
Like a special gift
From the Universe
Knowing that,
After this moment,
There will be none like it
Everything will be different
And that
Everything will be alright

March 8, 2020
Everett, Washington

**The Direction Of Potential**

West is the direction of potential
East is known for its people and past
So, I’ve said goodbye to the latter
In my life’s pursuit of the former
And I couldn’t be happier

March 8, 2020
Everett, Washington

**Keeping The World Inside**

The fear keeping the world inside
Supposedly safe and away
From the too-tiny threat
Too easily passed
From person-to-person
In every place we normally go

The fear intensely building
When I feel my allergies,
Still adjusting to this new state
And this budding new season,
Act up, making me think,
Stupidly and irrationally,
I'm now just a number
On the spiking daily tally
When it's actually nothing

The fear of the sickness
Spreading unchecked
Ceasing the old
And the already ill
Where they lay
Because they had
The doomed misfortune
To pass by someone
Who sneezed openly

March 28, 2020
Edmonds, Washington

The world has radically changed in the past few weeks. I look forward to the day when I can say, "Phew, thank goodness *that's* over!"

**The Distance Between Poems**

The distance between poems
Is by no means a gage
Or an indicator
Of action or inaction
On the part of the writer
Sometimes we're just busy
Living life and lack the ability
To notate or comment on it

March 28, 2020
Edmonds, Washington

**I'm Wholly Unimpressed**

I'm wholly unimpressed by
Those who are famous
Because people are people
Sure, some have jobs
That make them well-known
But they're not better
Than anyone else
Yes, I've gotten the phrase,
"Don't you know who I am?"
Lobbed in my direction
More than a few times
Usually from actors
Who I sort of recognize
But honestly couldn't name
Or identify what roles
They're actually known for
The kinds of people
You'd have to look up
On IMDB or Wikipedia
The kinds of people who turn
The taste of fame
Into a bitter mixture
They happily shove down
Everyone's mouth
Every chance they get
Thankfully, I am not
Starstruck in the least
And won't feed into
The endless desperation
Of their attention-needing
Bad-behavior ways

March 28, 2020
Edmonds, Washington

I don't know what prompted this.

Oh, I remember now. It popped into my mind that I've met a good number of celebrities due to the nature of my career, and how some of them were just dicks.

I should also add that most of them were also super nice.

**Pacific**

A warmer place
A different view
A different mindset
A complete 180
From what I've always known
Back when the sun over the water
Meant morning
Getting up
Getting going
The dawn of a new day
And now
I have changed
My place
My view
My vantage
Myself
As I face the brilliance of the setting sun
With my continent of experience
Contained, firmly back there,
In the growing darkness behind me
As I practice mindfulness
I've never previously known
Choosing to live in the moment
Appreciating and absorbing every detail
This Universe has graciously given me
In this place looking out over the Pacific
Where the silhouetted Olympics
Pierce and hold up the neon orange clouds
Backsplashed by the casually sliding sun
Who just wants to take a dip in the water
And slide around the other side of this planet
Which is completely fine by me
Since sunsets here seem to last for hours
And signify not the end of the day
But the beginning of the night
That is mine to enjoy

March 28, 2020
Edmonds, Washington

I LOVE standing in my backyard and seeing the ocean. The sunsets here are amazing.

**The Energy Is Here**

The energy is here
So why not use it
Instead of sitting,
Waiting passively
For things to match
Someone else's wants
Someone else's timeline
When you could be
Reaching, achieving
Your goals and desires
And living your best life

March 29, 2020
Edmonds, Washington

## Watching The Whitecaps

Watching the whitecaps
Grit, lighten the surface
Of the navy-hued table
Splaying out in the distance
Which was reflectively smooth
Earlier this very morning
But the weather has changed
And so has the moving light
Making this shifting canvas
Framed by the fir trees
More engrossing than TV

March 29, 2020
Edmonds, Washington

**Just One Purpose**

With untold trillions
Spent on “defense”
Over the past decades
The false protection
Could not save us
From an enemy
So simple and basic
Invisible and unseen
An enemy who
Knows nothing about
Borders or politics
Cares nothing about
Religion or gods
Is indifferent to
Our ruined economy
A virus who has
Just one purpose:
To spread

March 29, 2020
Edmonds, Washington

This is where capitalism has failed us. I read that years ago when SARS was dying out, research money for a coronavirus vaccine dried up because it was no longer deemed a threat. Basically, it wasn’t profitable. Imagine if they had created a coronavirus vaccine and we all had been inoculated – this current plague never would have happened.

# APRIL

**I Have Traded The Stars For The Sea**

I have traded all aspects of what I normally see
The snowy fields changing, growing with the seasons
For the sparkly islanded-in waters of the Sound

I have changed the birds that dot the sky
The gray pigeon-like mourning doves
For braying seagulls and gliding eagles

I have exchanged the frame that holds my view
The gently rolling Berkshire hills
For the rocky snow-capped Olympics

I have swapped the nighttime spectacle above
The brilliant rural display of infinite stars
For the lightshow of the city and boats below

I have traded the stars for the sea
Exchanging, upgrading my experience
Enriching my daily life with joy I've never known

April 12, 2020
Edmonds, Washington

Most of the poems just flow out of me quick and I have to keep up or else I'll lose my thoughts. This poem took about an hour to write and I changed the direction and form of it several times during the process, but I like where it ended up.

**It Must Be Tough To Be A Contrarian**

It must be tough to be a contrarian
To live in a knee-jerk world
Without reason or thought
Whose life is solely defined
By the things they don't like
It must be hard to be so negative
To be so against everything
Anyone enjoys or likes,
Unable to realize
We're all different
And hey, that's perfectly okay

April 12, 2020
Edmonds, Washington

I can't imagine choosing to be that angry all the time.

As a contrast to the last poem, I wrote this in three minutes.

**Humsmudge**

The low sound
Emanating
From the blurred
Table and chairs
Facing me
The very ones
That should be
Clear and quiet
And not moving
Afraid to touch
Whatever's going on
Fearing the unknown
Of the supernatural
Will I vanish
Through some portal?
Will I become one
With the humsmudge?
Will I burst into flames?
Will a cheesecake appear?
Should I trick someone else
To be the first to touch it?
I honestly don't know
But I feel like I can't
Take my eyes off of it
For fear it'll grow
Or it'll sneak up on me
Forcing me to face
The mystery head-on
Instead of from
A safe distance
Which is exactly
Where I'm heading now

April 25, 2020
Edmonds, Washington

## April

I had an idea for a short story about a table and chairs that just started vibrating and emitting a low humming sound while looking all blurry. What's the cause? What'll happen? I have no idea. Or, rather, I have too many ideas on where it could go. Since it's on my mind, I wrote a poem about it.

**The Years Are Getting Worse**

Every time the calendar
Goes from one year to the next
And we all take a moment
To relax and breathe
A collective sigh of relief
Until immediately
We're badly battered once again
By the terribleness of the times
In which we live
I've come to the realization
That the years are getting worse
Remembering the bad things
From back then and how now
They seem quaint in comparison
Like listening to a 2nd grader
Complaining about math class
While you're failing AP Calculus
And then I think a thought
That truly scares me:
What if in the future,
I look back on now
And laugh at how
Silly I was for thinking
How tough the times are
When, then,
Things are unimaginably worse
Just as now
Was impossible to predict
When living
In the better times

April 25, 2020
Edmonds, Washington

So impossible to predict…and I write science fiction for fun.

**Nature's Kiss Goodnight**

Every night
A watercolor
Being painted
And edited
In real time
In the sky, there,
Above the ocean,
Reflecting
On the windows
Of the condos
Surrounding me
Redirecting the light
Back to me
So I can see
The majesty
Of nature's
Kiss goodnight
Comforting
Letting us know
There is beauty
In the world

April 25, 2020
Edmonds, Washington

Diggity DANG, the sunsets here are beautiful. My Instagram feed is pretty much just sunsets now.

Well, it was pretty much just sunsets before I moved here as well, but *here*, wow, it's on a whole other level.

**To Take A Break**

I know I've mentioned this before
So there's no real need to say this
*…but…*
I feel like the point hasn't been made
That when we experience momentum
The for real and for true kind
Where awesome things keep rolling
One into another into another
Seemingly without end
Until
You decide to stop…
*Just for a minute*
You know, to take a break
Because you've done so much work
And you have! Wow, so much!
But the pause you take
Stops the momentum completely
Taking you out of the rhythm
Removing you from the flow
Halting the progress you've made
Cooling the engine powering you
Ending the productivity experienced
Preventing progress from happening
For the sake of some time off
Knowing that it's going to take
So impossibly long
To get things started
Revving, going
Once again
And who knows if you'll be able to
Reach the success you had before
Probably not
So…if I were you
I'd keep going
Just in case
Because you never know

April 25, 2020
Edmonds, Washington

**Being Still**

Being still
Being open
To the point
Where I am aware
Of everything
Around me
In my domain
And how it connects
With everything else
Feeling the interplay
Of energy
Back and forth
Surrounding, defining
Making it all known
Presence, intentions,
All of it
And how it all fits together
Perfectly, like a puzzle
Where all the pieces
Were specifically machined
To join together in a specific way
Sometimes in ways we never thought
Or intended, or considered
But that's ok
Because the Universe once had the foresight
To plan for this exact occurrence
And knew it would happen
Which is why
*CLICK*
It all snaps together
Like each piece
Was made for each other
Because it was
And taking this feeling
Of being connected
To every other piece
And spreading out

## April

Faster than light
Seeing all things
Spreading out from
The speck that is me
Encircling the whole world
And spreading out from
The speck that is the Earth
To the infinity past all sight
And everything contained within
Every time I quiet my mind
And choose to feel beyond

April 25, 2020
Edmonds, Washington

I quieted my mind, listened to Yo La Tengo's song, "The Story Of Yo La Tango [*sic*]," and just wrote.

**46**

46
Is one more than
45
Which is okay
Since that number
Is sullied, soiled,
Ruined for all time
And I am past it
And moving onward

April 30, 2020
Edmonds, Washington

Happy birthday to me!

April

# MAY

**A Better Path**

It's as if the Universe
Finally had enough
Frustration at watching
The lives on this planet
Be squandered chasing
Nothing but dollars
So, it hit the reset button
Casting aside,
Flushing away
How it had always been
And making us all
A little more aware
And introspective
Of ourselves
A little more aware
And considerate
Of others
And hopefully we all
Will learn and be
Changed from this
Massive experience
And thoughtfully choose
A better path

May 3, 2020
Edmonds, Washington

What are we meant to learn from all of this? How will things change? What will the new reality look like? I have some ideas, but I think the more interesting aspect is how we, as souls, will make use of the life lessons provided by this pandemic.

**Living Near The Ocean**

Living near the ocean offers
Something different
Like not just being on vacation
But living in it
Seeing the dynamic surface
Changing with the light
Moving with the wind
Mirroring the sky above
Reflecting the sunsets
Burning above the horizon
Cooling in the breeze
That traversed the sea
Just to greet
And welcome you
To this great place
At all hours
Of every day
You're here

May 16, 2020
Edmonds, Washington

**All The Protection**

Being old
And white
And male
Seems to be
All the protection
They think they need
From the virus
Ravaging the country
Because that group
Likes to eschew
All scientific guidelines
And put everyone else
Including themselves
In infectious danger by
Refusing to wear a mask

May 16, 2020
Edmonds, Washington

Seriously, if a person isn't wearing a mask, 80% of the time they're an old white male.

**Pivoting The Feelings**

I love how the day
Can completely change
From dark, drizzly gray
To bright, sunny yay
Before you've even noticed
Pivoting the feelings
Of everyone under the rainbow

May 16, 2020
Edmonds, Washington

**Every Shade Of Blue**

When you live by the sea
Throughout the day
You have, available to you,
Every shade of blue
You could ever hope to see
From the palest barely blue
Close to the horizon
To the brightest sky blue
Making up the height
Of the sky up above
To the rich undulating navy
Of the ocean below
And the nearly blackish blue
Dwindling well past sunset

May 16, 2020
Edmonds, Washington

**Blind Faith**

Blind faith
In the liar
Whose name
And image
You instantly know
Without further description
Or another word about them
Making devotees
Abandon reason and science
And thousands of years
Of empirical thought
Despite the conflictions
And outright fabrications
That a modicum of research
Would instantly prove false
But still the followers believe
Railing against their own interests
Hurting themselves in the process
Because being a contrarian
And "stickin' it" to others
Is held in the highest regard

May 16, 2020
Edmonds, Washington

**The Short Idea**

The short idea
The one you never knew was there
Until it pops up
Unknown until it made itself seen
Hard to ignore
Because it has true lasting power
Making you
Start to question everything
You've held
Close and dear to your heart
Like right now
Creating an inversion
Swapping what you knew
With what
Is now rising in your full view
Grabbing
Your attention in all the ways
You wish
Your old beliefs could do
But no
They just can't compete
With this
The short idea you never expected

May 16, 2020
Edmonds, Washington

What does it mean? I don't know. I cleared my mind and wrote while listening to "Untitled" from Interpol's *Turn On The Bright Lights* album. I wrote to the shape of one short line, one long line, which end up swapping with one another halfway through.

**The New Car Smell**

The new car smell
Is something that's neat
Because of what it represents
The new car look
Perfect and pristine
And in a condition
It will never see again
Once the ritual
Of daily living
Takes ahold
As the dust
The crumbs
And the fast food bags
Land and accumulate
Making what was new
Into something used

May 16, 2020
Edmonds, Washington

I bought a new car today.

**Your Time To Be A Sponge**

When you're young
The world is so limited
Just your home and family
And the immediate world
Begging to be explored

When you're old
The world shrinks small
Due to constant erosion
Removing the world you once knew –
Range, curiosity, ability, family

The time in-between –
That's when the world
Is yours to explore
Your time to be a sponge
And absorb every moment
Filling this life so completely full
That it's dense and heavy
So, when you squeeze it
The richness pours and flows
Like a waterfall of experience

May 23, 2020
Edmonds, Washington

While walking Baxter a few minutes ago it struck me that when we're young, our world is so tiny…and the same is true when we're really old. It's the decades in-between where it's so important to fill it with amazing experiences.

I wrote this while listening to Ryan Adams's wonderful cover of Taylor Swift's "Shake It Off" on repeat.

**An Incomprehensible Mess**

I came across the Instagram feed
Of someone I knew in school growing up
Unfortunately, often mistaken for a nerd
Based on his appearance
Not his grades
Or his abilities
Which were far from the label
Easily applied and hopelessly stuck
At too young of an age to escape.
In middle school,
He hit the contrarian stage
Which he never outgrew
And instead, made it
Central to his existence
Proud to be dickish
To everyone for any reason
He thrived on the attention
No matter how negative
And that's when I forgot him
Moving on with my own life.
Now, twenty-five years later,
Here I am looking at his photos
All 85,000 of them
Almost none are scenes,
Slices of life, showing
What he's been up to
Instead he left behind
An incomprehensible mess
Of right-wing memes created by Russians
For the consumption of the easily swayed
Bought hook, line, and sinker
Shared freely and instantly
Like it was his job
Which, in a way, it was
Because at some point
He had health issues,
And addiction issues,

Causing him to lose
His minimum wage job,
And somewhere in there
His wife left him
Taking his four kids,
And the only pictures
Showing his life
Were comment-less,
Like-less selfies
Showing an unsmiling him
Staring blankly,
Emotionless into the phone
With the only other information
Being the geotag he added
With the address
Of the homeless shelter
He was apparently staying at
These pictures showing
The weathered face
The stark reality
Of a man who had been stripped
Of everything he ever knew
Interspersed with right-wing memes
And text-pictures
Of him railing against "the libs"
And how the president
Has made America great
When clearly
Things couldn't be worse
And after about twenty minutes
Of continuous scrolling
And only going back
Less than a week
Through his postings
I stopped
And scrolled back up
To check the date of his last photo
Uploaded in mid-January
Meaning that something happened

## May

Because you don't go
From uploading hundreds a day
To nothing
Unless you died
Which is the only logical reason
Someone with that kind of compulsion
Would stop so suddenly and completely
If so, I hope he finally
Was able to find peace

May 23, 2020
Edmonds, Washington

**Blasts Of Colors**

The colors
Of the flowers
Have changed
My view immensely
Distracting me
Everywhere I go
Seeing blasts of color
Neon pinks
Popping purples
A tree of yellows
Whites with bees
Reds among greens
Changing the way
I see the season
From something
Merely in-between
To the main event

May 23, 2020
Edmonds, Washington

It is SO PRETTY here.

**It Is So Easy**

It is so easy
To get caught up
In the gross stuff
The crappy thoughts
Which, if focused on,
Will turn into an avalanche
Rumbling, racing down the mountain
Threatening and intending to bury you
Without a second thought
Because that's the job of negativity
Only if you choose to give it your attention
Because where you focus your energy
Is so insanely powerful
You can choose to be overwhelmed
By all of the shitty things in life
Most of which you have no control over
Or you can look for the good things
That are right here, right in front of you
The beauty, the positivity
The awesome things you can appreciate
And express gratitude for
When you choose to spend your energy
On things that make you happy
It's amazing how quickly it can turn around

May 23, 2020
Edmonds, Washington

**You've Run Out Of Road**

That gravitational pull
Bringing you out West
The journey wished for
Occupying so much space
In your mind and heart
For so many years
After so many months
Preparing for this trip
And thousands of miles
Driven over too few days
You've run out of road
Ending here at the coast
Where the land dips and
Slides under the Pacific
And you allow yourself
A chance to pause
For a minute,
Or a month, to stop
And appreciate the beauty
That's excessively abundant
Everywhere you look here
And realize the ideal town
You've always wanted
Does actually exist
And you're already in it

May 30, 2020
Edmonds, Washington

I started this poem with the notion of people who are drawn to "go West," but what happens when you run out of "West" because there's a big ocean sitting there? I think they either turn around and go back home, or they like what they've found and stay.

It took me a really long time to write it and, at one point, I had lines about orca whales being happy to eat you if you ventured too far out into the water, or some silliness like that.

**Enjoy The Superficial View**

The ocean may look pretty
But it's deep
And dark
Meaning things are hidden
Nasty hungry things
With teeth to eat me
Some of them are squishy
And others are very monstery
Which is why I like to stay safe
Here, on the land,
And enjoy the superficial view
Of the flat wavy, reflect water
While enjoying deep thoughts
About land-based, happy things
Trying not to think about
All the stuff under the surface
Wanting me to come down
For an extended visit
To show me around
Just in time for dinner

May 30, 2020
Edmonds, Washington

Stuff that lives under the water freaks me out.

Not seals. They're cute.

**The Regressive Bygone**

As a society
I thought we were cultured
I thought we had grown up
And learned from our mistakes
In our embarrassingly awful past
While most of us have evolved
Others resisted, desperately clinging
Clutching, to the regressive bygone
By the throats of those they deemed
Less than equal for no real reason
Other than the hateful ways learned
From the graying, dying generations
Struggling to hold onto the power
They never had to begin with
By murdering their neighbors
They will quickly discover
That the hugely vast majority
Of everyone in this country
Are united, hand-in-hand,
Humanity unified together
Against hatred and racism
Whenever it may arise

May 30, 2020
Edmonds, Washington

**Pole Dance**

On the fishing pier
Enjoying the sunset
When I looked to the left
Along the long railing
And saw the intricate
Pole dance engaged in
By those fishing –
The whip, whip, flick
As the lines were cast out
From one to the next
Onward down the pier
Much like the "the wave"
Done by a stadium crowd
But on a much smaller scale
With much different intentions
By those hoping to catch
And those just using this
As an excuse to get out
And enjoy some quiet time
Alone with the others
In this special place

May 30, 2020
Edmonds, Washington

May

# JUNE

**This Moment**

Shutting out all external noise
Focusing inward on myself
Who I am and
What I am to become
The person I am growing into
Because anyone
Who has stopped growing
Might as well go to the cemetery
And bury themselves right now
For they have stopped living
And chosen to not become more
Than the mote they are now
Why else are we here
If not to experience,
Grow, and expand
As human beings
So, take this time
And choose to live
Making a difference
Because this moment
Is gone
As soon as you live it

June 6, 2020
Edmonds, Washington

**Bumperless**

The loud bang
The quick crunching
Of plastic and metal
Breaking the quiet normalcy
Causing everyone
Living within earshot
To leap to their feet
And look outside
At the car askew
In the road strewn
With a car bumper
And dozens of
Broken plastic bits
While the other car
Poking halfway out
Their driveway
Sat bumperless
As a result of being
Careless
With pulling out
Onto the street
And not looking
To see if anyone
Was coming
Making us all
Stand and survey
The scene
Of the accident
Where no one was injured
Except for the wallets
Of those directly involved

June 6, 2020
Edmonds, Washington

This just happened ten minutes ago. Amazingly, a police car happened to be driving down the hill and was on the scene ten seconds after it happened.

**I Don't Mind The Rain**

I don't mind the rain
When it's also sunny
Getting the best of everything
The freshness of the falling shower
With that pure clean smell
That detergent companies
Can never seem to replicate
And the faint dampness
Cooling and refreshing
Like at the supermarket
When the misters spray
In the vegetable section
While the warmth radiates
Downward from the sun
Still shining despite it all
And half the visible sky
Is that radiant hue of blue
That we crave to see
Reminding us of the finest days
We've ever known
Belonging to our best memories

June 6, 2020
Edmonds, Washington

## Nosy Neighbor

The retired man
Living next door
Is quite actively
A nosy neighbor
Peering in windows
Inspecting my trash
Making sure I don't
Take up too much room
In the recycling bins
Standing in my yard
Looking around
Always looking
Mentally measuring
And taking notes
Filing them away
For some future
When he might
Need them for
Something
Some reason
I don't know why
Maybe I've become
His project
His hobby
Occupying his time
His bandwidth
Causing me to
Close my blinds
Making him
Even more curious
As to what I could
Possibly be doing
In my apartment

June 6, 2020
Edmonds, Washington

What am I doing? Right now, I'm writing about him.

Ha ha! He literally just looked in my window as I typed that.

## Adventure Happens

Adventure happens
When you're from
Somewhere else
Going to someplace
You've never been
Doing something
Completely new

June 14, 2020
Edmonds, Washington

Or…adventure happens when you Instagram it.

**The Year Of The Hunker**

2020 is the year
Of the hunker
As we settle in
And down
Away and
Hopefully safe
From the virus
And the danger
Lurking out there
Trying its best
To suffocate
Every last one of us
We must remember
To not fall for
The American mindset
And completely forget
About the problem
After a few weeks
So, for this to be
Going on for months
Is beyond the patience
Of most everyone
As they shrug off
And completely dismiss
The risk of the pandemic
So they can get dinner
At a restaurant or a haircut
Instead of staying in
Where it's safe
Where I am
Because I
Listen to the scientists
And I do not forget
So easily for the sake
Of minor inconveniences
And I will ensure
I will be safe

Throughout all of this

June 14, 2020
Edmonds, Washington

**The Time Of Alignment**

The time of alignment
Is approaching
As the number
Of strange coincidences
Is increasing
The things impossible to ignore
Or brush off
That keep on piling up
Each and every one
Clamoring for
Demanding your full attention
One after another
Boom Boom Boom
Each one sending full body chills
Up and down your skin
Because of how close
They hit home
And how much
They resonate
With what you know to be true
And with what you most want
With each tick
With each case
You get closer
As the momentum
Brings them faster
Until the inevitable moment,
You knew was coming
But told yourself
You weren't prepared for,
Arrives

June 14, 2020
Edmonds, Washington

**The Echoing Fuzzy**

The echoing fuzzy
Indistinct and inarticulated
That, at first,
Seemed so disjointed
Became rhythmic
With its timing
And its continuing
Which, at first,
Repulsed, but then
Became interesting
A thing craved
For its departure
From the daily norm
As it buzzed its way
Through the silence
Into some deep place
Changing opinions
Changing directions
Of those who connect
With its sweet sound

June 14, 2020
Edmonds, Washington

I was listening to “Barnaby, Hardly Working” by Yo La Tengo and was inspired.

**Temporary Is Not A Sustainable Modality**

Temporary is not
A sustainable modality
Or a reasonable way to live
So, freely toss and destroy
Anything inflatable or
Held together fleetingly
Making the conscious choice
For durability and permanence
Be a choosy purchaser
Making sure, much like you,
What you surround yourself with
Is also truly meant to last

June 14, 2020
Edmonds, Washington

**To The Surface Again**

Each week
I work
A little more
On the huge poem
Meant to encapsulate
This dumpster of a year
But each week
It gets worse
Making what I wrote
Seem out of date
Out of touch
With the complexity
And the severity
Of the times
So, I delete lines
And add lines
With more
Forceful phrasing
Detailed picturing
Trying to demonstrate
The shitshow
Raging around
Like the ravenous monster
Threatening to consume us all
So, I hunker down
A little deeper
And update my words
Each and every week
Until someday
This will all be done
And the monster will be gone
And the sunlight brings
All of us to the surface again

June 14, 2020
Edmonds, Washington

The song, “The Sun” by The Naked And Famous came on as I was finishing the poem, “Temporary Is Not A Sustainable Modality,” and I immediately started writing this one even though I hadn’t even saved the last one yet. It was one of those moments when my brain is so hooked on the momentum of the music that I plow through and write.

**To Wear A Mask**

Defiantly contrarian
To the point where
If someone says
To wear a mask
For your own safety
And those around you
You take the opportunity
To stick it to them
How dare they try
And take your liberty
And your freedom
By saying you should
Wear a mask
A simple thing
That will literally
Stop you from
Inadvertently killing
Those that you love
Because you were
Too stubborn to listen
Because when you
Finally feel regret
It will be too late

June 20, 2020
Edmonds, Washington

I am beyond astounded that wearing a mask during a global pandemic is seen as a “political” issue.

**The Ones Without**

I wonder what
Life lessons
Those defiant souls
Are here to learn
The ones without
A shred of
Common sense
The ones without
A thought or care
About anyone else
The ones who
Can only say
"Me first,"
Immediately,
Always, and
At all costs
The ones who
Go through life
Like a bulldozer
Blasting through
Whatever's in their way
Without regard,
Remorse, or reflection

June 20, 2020
Edmonds, Washington

**A Bankable Given**

Living there was once
A bankable given
With five colleges
In the immediate area
You could open anything
Catering to the students
And be wonderfully successful
But no one ever imagined this –
A time when a microscopic virus
Would decimate economies
Forcing most everything
You know and loved
To shut their doors for good
To put more people out of work
Than the Great Depression
Could have ever dreamed,
With everything changing
And now talk of colleges closing
I can't imagine how life there
Can ever hope to recover

June 20, 2020
Edmonds, Washington

I've been thinking about the Pioneer Valley of western Massachusetts, where I recently moved here from. With the Five Colleges there (UMass, Amherst, Smith, Mount Holyoke, and Hampshire) that area seemed like the perfect place to weather any economic downturn. There will always be students. They will always have money. Everything will be fine…until the students stopped coming. And suddenly, there was no more money. Now everything there is closing. I think about it a lot, how crazy fortunate I was to have gotten a job out in the Pacific Northwest and to have gotten out of the Valley at the exact perfect moment. It's pretty crazy how things happen like that.

I also spend a lot of time thinking about the Berkshires, where I'm originally from, and how their entire economy is based on tourism…and how all of the massive summer activities that carry businesses through the entire year are not opening this year, and what the impact will be. It's so scary.

**A Release**

As the followers assemble
For a mass celebration
Of the worst aspects of America
The fact they have to sign
A release saying they won't hold
The man or his reelection campaign
Responsible for contracting
The virus is beyond telling
That they know the risks
And are afraid of being sued
By giving the virus
Exactly what it needs:
Easy, unfettered access
To the perfect population –
Mask-less, older, overweight,
And angry, with all of them
Yelling – spitting mad
About all of the people
Who refuse to let them
Keep America great,
While enclosed and confined
Like a pressure cooker petri dish
In near-ideal conditions for
Simmering, spreading the sickness
Like a fire, smoldering, and catching
Before they bring the heat home
And the bonfire of disease
Spreads and consumes
Those who refused to believe
It could be anything more
Than fake news

June 20, 2020
Edmonds, Washington

I feel bad for all of the thousands of people who come into contact with the rally-goers and will die because of their stubborn refusal to wear a mask (and avoid crowded places). I saw in the news that a lot of these people are pointing to the Black Lives Matter protests and saying, “They’re not socially distancing and no one is saying that’s wrong.” Well, yes, officials have been saying being in rallies is not a good idea, but at least nearly all of the BLM protesters are wearing masks, whereas nearly none of the Trump supporters are wearing masks. Big difference.

**Foil To The Land**

The massive mirror
In the distance
The living, moving
Foil to the land
Whitecapping
But still reflecting
The conditions above
A lighter and brighter
Hue of blue
A drabber shade of gray
A patchwork middle
White and indigo
Or a messy spill
Of sunset orange
Always changing
Always different
Always amazing
Always appreciated

June 20, 2020
Edmonds, Washington

I felt after the last few poems dealing with the craziness that's been going on in the world, it would be nice to write about nature. Thanks, ocean!

**Hate Corner**

The house sitting
One block from the water
Prominently at an intersection
The house with the iron fence
The kind that people have installed
As a way to say, “Stay away”
Wrapping around the property
Meant to keep others out
In this very friendly town
The one with all the signs
Commanding *NO TRESSPASSING*
And the other proclamations
About gays being an abomination,
And demanding we lock up Hillary
Years after that was a thing
Crazy people once parroted,
And another calling for
The public to boycott an airline
That had fired the homeowner
Twenty-something years prior
Which must be a troubling chip
On his shoulder since this sign
Is wired with electricity
And illuminated at night.

Between the terrible fence
And the nondescript house
Is the abnormally large yard
Large enough for two houses
But empty, flat, and evenly green
Severely mowed into “perfection”
The kind of landscaped crew-cut
That Hank Hill would approve of
Completely devoid
Of any personality or character.

This property,

Which is locally known
As "Hate Corner"
Sits in stark contrast
With every one of its neighbors
Encircled on all sides,
Surrounded by color
As everyone else uses their yards
To celebrate the diversity
And vivid color of nature
As plants, shrubs, bushes, and flowers
Of every size, shape, and color
Dazzle, burst, and impress
The passers-by
With how beautiful
This town truly is
And show that the soul
Of an area is not defined
By the darkest parts

June 27, 2020
Edmonds, Washington

The guy who owns this house actually wrote a letter to the editor of the local paper complaining how people just need to stay away from Edmonds, because it's attracting too many artists and creative types.

**Aggressively Orange**

This group of flowers
Growing right here
On this random corner
Is being overly bright
And aggressively orange
Clearly showing off
And trying to upstage
Those other flowers
Growing over there
Who don't like to be
Braggy, or overly showy
But being meek like that
Will never get you bees
Swarming to pollinate you
Or stop people in their tracks
So they can take your picture
Unless you're bold with color
Living to be remembered

June 27, 2020
Edmonds, Washington

@sarahladuke posted a photo of tiger lilies (?) on her Instagram account and said, "So aggressively orange = perfect." I liked the phrase and ran with it.

**From Here To There**

The distance between
Here and there
Seems, at times, unbridgeable
An impossible distance
Separating us
From what we know now
To what we've always dreamt –
Apprehensively, cautiously, just in case
It was ever to somehow happen
And life would become unbearable
With overwhelming joy
But that's the best-case scenario
So far away from where we stand
In the middle of the worst year
Like a child, whose socked feet
Are sunken into the cushion,
Staring at the lava-covered floor
Wondering how they'll get
From the couch to the safety
Of the cool tiles of the kitchen
With the coffee table missing
Removing hope of safe passage
Necessitating another way –
Forming new beliefs
Of being stronger
Of being fireproof
Of believing in possibility
Of bridging the gap
Imagining crossing the span
As if it were like nothing at all
Like walking across the floor
Fearlessly, easily
From here to there
Reaching the dreams
And living that better life now

June 27, 2020

June

Edmonds, Washington

I recently joined a writer's group in Edmonds, called, EPIC Group Writers (I've always personally liked the word "Epic" because it looks so much like "Eric"). This month they had a writing contest asking members to submit prose or poetry with the subject of "the distance between." I thought about submitting my poem, "Equidistant" from 2018, but the maximum length for poetry submissions is only 40 lines, and that poem is something like 100+ lines. So, I whipped up something new, because that's what I do.

Note: I won the writing contest with this poem.

**Tilt**

Resting.
Creating.
Opposites:
One
Necessary,
Both
Enjoyable.
Options
Predilections
Weighed
Weighted
Leaning
Toward
One
Over
The
Other
Trying
Not
To
Tip
Over
Balance
Without
Overdoing
Without
Falling
Without
Failing
Trying
Maintaining
A
Happy
Medium
With
A
Slant

Mirroring
Earth's
Axial
Tilt
Creating
Seasons
Creating
Contrast
Enabling
Delicious
Situations
With
Each
Degree
Further
Out
Where
Increased
Pitch
Lessens
Yawns
Amplifying
The
Dangerous
Possibility
Of
Eventually
Tipping
Too
Far
When
Safety
Evaporates
And
Falling
Or
Flying
Is
The

## Only
## Option

June 27, 2020
Edmonds, Washington

Trying something a little different.

**Is The Same As The Gray**

The gray of the clouds
Is the same
As the gray
Of the distant mountains
Is the same
As the gray
Of the nearby hills
Is the same
As the gray
Of the choppy ocean
Is the same
As the gray
Of the drizzle falling
Is the same
As the gray
Of the cars on the street
Is the same
As the gray
As the cat on my couch
Is the same
As the gray
Of the ashes in the fireplace
Is the same
As the gray
Of the mood in my heart

June 27, 2020
Edmonds, Washington

Actually, I'm in a great mood, but the ending went with the rest of the poem. You have to continue the momentum while you're in it.

# JULY

**Super Slouching**

Super slouching
On the oversized couch
On a lazy Saturday
Until I fell asleep
And an hour later
I woke up with a pain
In a specific part
Of my chest
With each breath
Causing my mind
To go immediately
To the worst
Wondering if
I've been infected
And it spiraled
As I panicked
And planned
A trip to get tested
And wondered
What I'd do about work
Until I sat up
And burped
Ending the pain
And the freak-out
Because it was just
Trapped gas

July 11, 2020
Edmonds, Washington

Gee whiz, I was really mentally panicking there for a while.

Stupid coronavirus.

**Plain And Boring**

I remember when
Simple things
Like snacks
And sodas
Amped up their marketing
And they all became “Extreme”
But with a weird spelling
So it could be trademarked
And suddenly everything
Was heightened, extra,
And flavor-blasted
And nothing was normal anymore
Because it was plain and boring

Looking back on things
From this vantage point
That 2020 has given us
I think we all would choose
Anything average and normal
Because we are all sick
Of being tossed about on this
Never-ending roller coaster
Of going from one extreme
To another; instantly and daily

July 11, 2020
Edmonds, Washington

“A regular taco with a regular soda, please.”
“Do you want that taco FLAVOR BLASTED or the soda to be X-TREEM™?”
“No, thank you. Just regular.”

**The Year That Aged Us**

Being human,
We are conditioned by our past
Learning how society works
Knowing what to expect
We figured out how
Everything fits together
And we go from there
Until we hit this year –
The year that aged us
More than any has before
As emergencies stacked on top
Of tragedies and were multiplied
By calamities, again and again
More and more, over and over
Stretching days into months
And months into decades
While forcing us to skip,
Postpone, or completely abandon
Our dear traditions, celebrations –
Anything resembling normalcy
While remaining indoors
Hunkering down with our fear
And extreme boredom as our minds
Continuously wander and wonder
Will things go back to normal, if ever?
And then to watch those who tried
Defiantly, to return to the old ways
Only to find themselves, weeks later,
Life-dependent on a ventilator
Causing the cowering to deepen
And the fear of others to grow
As we batten down the hatches
And hope for a fresh start next year

July 11, 2020
Edmonds, Washington

May we all be able to make it to see the blue sky and sunny days of normalcy again.

I've been working on this poem, in one shape or another, for about two months now. When I read over what I had previously written, I found a very long, epic poem that spotlighted each detail and shitty aspect to this year, getting very specific, but I wasn't happy with it. It felt like a fifty-foot tall Jenga game that was drunkenly teetering and ready to fall on top of me. I took the phrase "the year that aged us" out of that poem and started from scratch with this one.

**Repeated Exposure To Joy**

When the newsfeed
Gets too overpowering
Gets too overwhelming
Gets too depressing
And blasts you with sadness
Close the computer
Turn off the TV
Leave the phone behind
Walk out the door
Find a park, a view,
A place filled with beauty
Or even just a single flower
And focus on that
Feeling the terrible feelings
Flow out and be replaced
With peace and breathing
With happiness and smiles
With pure and good feelings
Making sure to stay longer
Than you would normally
And return more often
Than you think necessary
Because this is how you
Repair yourself and get better –
Repeated exposure to joy

July 11, 2020
Edmonds, Washington

## There Is A Reverence With The Process

There is a reverence with the process
With how I set aside the time
With how I squirrel myself away
With the lighting of the candle
Specifically chosen for this activity
Then the choosing of the playlist
Meant to inspire my creativity
Putting on the headphones
To block out everything else
Keeping me firmly in my world
Opening Microsoft Word
And driving my keyboard
Across the blank, snowed-in page
Filling it fully
With the twelve-point
Times New Roman
Of who I am
In this moment
Here
Not later
Not in the future
But right now
Leading me
(and, you)
To discover
And better understand
The magic of all things

July 15, 2020
Edmonds, Washington

**The Captain Of The Boat**

The captain of the boat
Listing severely
Capsizing
Clearly immanently
Going down
In a matter of time
Sooner than safety
Is busy yelling
Blaming others
Who had nothing to do
With the charting,
Steering, or anything
Is spending the last moments
Not working to help
Not trying to avert the crisis
Not even offering even a hand
As his arms are folded
Tightly across his chest
Matching the hateful glare
And the childish pouting
While constantly spouting
About inane things
Having nothing to do
With the catastrophe
Unfolding all around
Affecting everyone
About to slip under
Due to his dereliction

July 15, 2020
Edmonds, Washington

**Give Whales Space**

I saw a sign
In the window
At the convenience store
Showing a boat and an orca
Saying *Give Whales Space*
And I thought, “Okay”
So, I opened a wormhole
And sent them to orbit
Around Jupiter for a while
Which, I found out later,
They did not actually want
Because, as it turns out,
The whales did not
Put the sign up to begin with –
I don’t know who did,
But they should have talked
With the whales to begin with
If they had, they would have known
That the whales just wanted
A few thousand gallons of ice cream

July 19, 2020
Edmonds, Washington

True story.

**Watching The News**

Trying not to get mad
Watching the news
Because every day
The intensity
Seems to ratchet up a notch
The stupidity
Doubles down on yesterday
The audacity
Is breathtaking in scope
The brutality
Is truly terribly shocking
And even though I know
Tomorrow it will be worse
I still look to see
What's happened
In this world
That once seemed okay
That's since gone wrong

July 19, 2020
Edmonds, Washington

## Inspired By The Movement

Inspired by the movement
Pushed by the momentum
Bringing me to new heights
Places never before known

July 19, 2020
Edmonds, Washington

**Generations Removed**

As a society
We are many
Generations removed
From the faded history
And the older among us
Can only remember
The brightest parts
Whitewashed by time
The fondest memoires
They choose to re-live,
Rerun, over and over,
But conveniently forget
The tougher truths
The terrible times
They also lived through
In doing so, they deny
So many contemporaries
The same experiences
The same celebrated history
That was conveniently
And carefully swept under
The filthy welcome mat
That's now unreadable
And purposely off-putting
Meant to discourage
And actively turn away
Instead of ushering them within
The decaying, divided house
Proudly chanted as being
"Number one"

July 19, 2020
Edmonds, Washington

**I've Gone Over My Time Limit**

I've gone over my time limit
I said one hour
And now it's an hour and twelve
Meaning I went over
By a full twenty percent
But I noticed I'm still not stopping
I don't know why
It's not that I have anything
More to say
Or profound things to add
To the conversation
(the one-way conversation
 that's had when one writes
 and one reads what's been written)
Maybe I'm just not
In a stopping place
Or, possibly I'm done
But these words were
What was leftover in my fingers
Like the water still in a garden hose
After the spigot was turned off
Still ready to flow and soak
Anyone there, unaware,
Who's made the mistake
Of unwittingly handling it
That's what's going on here
Between me and you
Or, at least *was* going on
Until this moment
When I stopped

July 19, 2020
Edmonds, Washington

**Get Some Water In Your Eyes**

Living near the ocean
Changes your priorities
Makes you crave getting out
To get some water in your eyes
To have the need to see the sea
Driving to the edge of the map
Where the map lady in your phone
Tells you to go anywhere but there
Where the horizon planes
The razor-lined space
Between the baby blue above
And the wavy blue below
While watching the setting sun
Leaving you stunned
With its glorious goodbye
To the receding day

July 28, 2020
Edmonds, Washington

Kari inspired this poem by saying the phrase that I titled the poem after.

# AUGUST

**Dandelions**

Like dandelions
Spreading across the continent with ease
Making the land from sea to sea
A fresh carpet of yellow
Before turning white with death
And flying off to spread further
With nothing here to hold it back
Or block it from spreading
Just strong emotions about concepts
It knows and cares nothing about
Because nature does what nature does:
Finds the ideal environment
Replicates, and repeats – again and again
Regardless of what the host thinks
As they actively aid in the spreading
Doing exactly what's needed
To move it along to fresh pastures
That will soon be covered
Completely with dandelions

August 1, 2020
Edmonds, Washington

People who refuse to wear masks are the worst kinds of people. It's like they're actively *trying* to spread the virus. I thought how dandelions spread across America so easily and completely due to their not being any natural enemies here was an apt metaphor for what's going on right now with the virus.

**Laundromat**

Sitting in the local laundromat
Reporting on what my eyes see
From the knowing perch of experience
As my first job was working in a laundry
From the ages of fourteen to nineteen
I went there after school and on weekends
Working, reading books, earning money,
In a place that had pride in its appearance
In a place that was comfortable and nice –
Unlike this laundry I'm in right now
Looking up at the stained ceiling tiles
Crinkled from years of the cycle
Getting wet, drying, and repeating.

Next to that, the exposed light tubes
Dirty and often working alone
Instead of being in pairs
Like the fixture had intended
But instead, the owner decided
To save money, only one was needed.

Looking down at the sad gray carpet
Worn, thin, and threadbare,
Dappled with years of stains,
Unevenly cut in places
Where there was once
Something else, but is now gone.

Up to the exposed concrete walls
In three different colors
Like Neapolitan ice cream
But instead of distinct flavors
We got various ages of wall stages:
Naked gray, pink, and a yellowed white
Other areas are just unpainted drywall
Spaced evenly with nail-head dots.

In front of which sat a collection
Of old lamps and end tables
Stacked, forgotten,
And no longer seen by the owners
Near panels of plywood
For some long-planned project
Never realized, as whispered by
The thick layer of cobwebs and dust.

Over to my left is the change machine
Fitted with a hand-written sign
Declaring that, due to the change shortage,
To get quarters from the counter
As if there's a difference between
Dispensing from human and a machine.

Up again, there's a random wire
Electrical in nature, without a plug or end,
Hanging from the ceiling
Like a thick snake escaping
The ringed, water-stained tiles.

Over on the dryer to my right
Several signs each saying the same thing
But using different fonts and words
Warning not to leave machines unattended.

A cart hiding under a table glowered at me
Clearly decades-old, and an obvious hand-me-down
From one laundry to the next, until it landed here
Designed way too-low, with well-worn wheels
Below dents and streaks of rust on the legs
And the 70s ocher yellow paint worn off all edges
Form hundreds of thousands of hands
Grabbing and pushing loads of clothes
From here to there and back
Only to be bumped against a wall
Or rolled under a table for folding
When used, left, and forgotten.

The only new things I could see
Were a large washer
Which clearly replaced another
Much larger washer
Judging by the open hole on the wall
Showing the previous occupant's footprint
And the huge high-definition television
Looking strange and out of place
Beside the oversized "vintage"-looking wall clock.

The other patrons were quiet
Some with their masks on properly
Some with their noses exposed
Silently watching their clothes
Dancing and spinning rhythmically
As swirls of color in the dryer
Distinguishable from one another
Based on the owner's contents
Intimately known by only them.

The only movement discerned
During this waiting time phase
Was the frequent darting of eyes
From the clothes to the timer
To see how long was left of this
Forced meditative contemplation.

Occasionally there were instances
Where the people did not adhere
To the rules of the signage
As dryers stopped to a terrible chorus
Of one-note electronic wailing
Warning nobody present
That their clothes were done
With their happy dancing
And instead cooled while waiting
For their owners to finish cigarettes
Inhaled in the parking lot

Or return from some other errand.

I sat and did the same eye-dart
Until the number *01*
Finally reached *00*
Amid the familiar chiming
Setting my movements into motion
To collect my things
And leave this place.

August 3, 2020
Edmonds, Washington

A couple of weeks ago I had to wash a comforter that was too large to fit in our tiny washer and dryer. The laundry was in a nearby city and was pretty big. This is a description of what I saw from my seat.

**More Is A Mindset Beyond**

To feel the perfection
Of the words click
Solidly into place
Like plastic toy bricks
Building something
Bigger, lasting longer
Than the writer
Than the reader
Becoming something
Bigger than we ever
Thought possible
Than the current
Position we occupy
Than even the dreams
The big ones
We always fall back on
Because "more"
Is a mindset beyond
The treadmilling place
We occupy right now
*Here*, always, and forever
Isn't enough for me
More. I want more. Always –
That's where the future lives

August 7, 2020
Edmonds, Washington

I've been mildly tinkering with my next novel, *2493: The Death Of Bryn Struse* for a few years now. I've got about 60-something pages done, but haven't done real writing, beyond notes, or detailed notes, for a very long time. Today I sat down and wrote nearly eight pages and it felt effortless and amazing. Doing the thing you were placed on this planet, in this life, to do feels amazing – like everything is clicking into place.

**Evolutionary Point**

This messed up place
We've found ourselves in
Is a rare and powerful
Evolutionary point
Where we, as a people,
Are being pushed
In a direction, forward,
To make us grow
Whether we want to
Or flat out refuse
Either way we all
Will come out of this
Changed completely
From our economy
To our personalities
And everything in between
So, our choice is this:
Either we grow up
Or we will stop
But no one here
Will remain unchanged
From this year defined
By optical clarity

August 8, 2020
Edmonds, Washington

20/20 indeed.

**Focus On The Speck**

Larger than comprehension
Beyond discernable scope
The Universe is fathomless
And impossible to take in
So, focus on the speck
Where you find yourself now
And when that's in alignment
Spread your positive energy
Outward and upward
Impacting your place
In a joyous way
Making everything better
By just being here

August 8, 2020
Edmonds, Washington

**Choosing To Grow**

Thinking about the past
And all the routines
I've historically done
But also realizing
That keeps me in a place
Limiting my reach
Preventing me
From advancing
In this moment
Sure, I could do
All those things
Going through the motions
Until I reached this point
Right here,
When I'm stopping
And I'm saying "No."
And instead, making
The conscious decision
Choosing to grow
Into something new
Something beyond
What I used to be
Just last year
What I used to be
Just last week
Something beyond
Something better

August 8, 2020
Edmonds, Washington

I wrote this while listening to "Whiteout Conditions" by The New Pornographers.

**Truly Terrifying**

The blind faith of the followers
Who defiantly rebuffed considering
Facts, science, or rational thought
Are what I find to be truly terrifying
Refusal to be open to anything
That rests outside their narrow view
And against any kind of change…
The very things that actually move
Our society and humanity forward

August 11, 2020
Edmonds, Washington

If we didn't move forward, we'd still be in the Middle Ages. Change is a good thing. Opening one's worldview is a good thing.

**Noticed The Southern Movement**

Each night I watch the sunset
Because here, it's a spectacle
That's never to be missed
But lately, I've noticed
The Southern movement
As the place where the Sun
Chooses to make it's exit
Below the visible plane
Is a little further to the left
Each and every night
And I wonder where
It'll be leaving
Given a month
And how much earlier
It'll be getting darker
Which makes me sad
So, I make certain
That I appreciate
Every sunset
That swings on by

August 11, 2020
Edmonds, Washington

**Seeing The Smooth Orange Tinting**

Seeing the smooth orange tinting
Of the past-sunset light silhouetting
The purple Olympic range jutting
Above the Pacific waters lapping
Lightly against the active shore
Filled with families walking
Happily enjoying the scenery
With the day gently cooling
Breezily blowing the ocean air
Cementing summer memories
And making the scene complete

August 14, 2020
Edmonds, Washington

Such a nice evening on Olympic Beach in Edmonds, watching The Bubble Man make huge bubbles that lazily floated in the post-sunsetting light.

**The Tattered Scraps Of Your Present Self**

After all the color
Has fully and completely
Drained from the day
Is when the thoughts,
Normally chased away
By the Sun's bright light
And the increased distractions
Available during those hours,
Creeps back into the corners
Of the mind, of the heart,
And press the rewind button
Reviewing scenes best left
Firmly alone, in the past,
Thankfully forgotten,
Until they're remembered
And have you for company
Before their teeth are bared
And they have you for dinner
Until there is nothing left
Except the tattered scraps
Of your present self

August 14, 2020
Edmonds, Washington

I listened to "Untitled" by Interpol, felt the echoing darkness of the song as well as the darkness of the night outside and just wrote. I don't know what it means.

After the first two poems I wrote this month ("Dandelions" and "Laundromat"), I thought it might be fun to write every poem this month with a single-world title. I think that went away with the past few wordy-titled poems.

**Bringing The Universe Closer**

Quieting the mind
Closing the eyes
Focusing on what's beyond
This terribly dense
Physical world we inhabit
And going where I want
With meditation

Quieting the light
Opening the eyes
Focusing on what's beyond
This terrible, beautiful
Planet we're bound to
And going where I want
With telescopes

With both cases
I'm actively working on
Bringing the Universe closer
Looking inward
And looking out
And amazingly,
Coincidentally arriving at
The exact same place

August 14, 2020
Edmonds, Washington

**The Rhythm Of Life**

There is a beauty
To the rhythm of life
The ebbs and flows
The highs, the lows,
The getting old
The love, the lost,
The terrible cost
The scenic views
The messes we choose
The bundled pile
Spanning for miles
Making up this heap
Into which we keep
Our memories
And feelings
Combining into one
Over and over
Until we're done
And move on and in
To the world beyond
Only to do it all again
And hop right back in
So very enthusiastically

August 14, 2020
Edmonds, Washington

Fun fact: I can never ever spell "rhythm" correctly. I think it's the lack of vowels that messes me up. I keep wanting to put Es in there.

## Up Early For A Saturday

Up early for a Saturday
But still much later
Than any weekday
Outside looking up
At the bright blue
While feeling the air
So refreshing and cool
Holding onto the idea
That, here, in this moment
Possibility is all-encompassing
And I can do anything
With this day that I choose

August 15, 2020
Edmonds, Washington

But *will I* still remains to be seen. I'll report back later.*

*Note: I might not do this.

**The Little Personality**

Ridiculously oversized pickup trucks
Fulfill the need for one's inner bully
To be the center of attention
To command respect
To make everyone look up at them
To feel bigger than others
To give the impression they're important
To insinuate this much truck is actually needed
To intimidate anything and anyone smaller
To flaunt something that's just not there
To threaten with aggressive driving
To take up more room than necessary
To be insulated and above it all
To feel powerful
But in reality, they're afraid
And use this truck as a means
To cover and compensate
For the little personality
That can't manage their way
Through the day
Without feeling the need
To prove to strangers
That they're tough
And a man's man

August 15, 2020
Edmonds, Washington

The size of some of these trucks is laughably ridiculous – and then they jack them up even higher and need ladders to get in them. There's one in our area that is so big, it can't fit into a normal parking space (length or width) and the guy has to park it on the sidewalk.

**The Good Old Days**

Despite the nightmares
This year has conjured up for us
I still maintain a sense of optimism
And have hope
That things will improve
For society as a whole
Or…
I could be completely wrong
And we're click-click-clicking
Up the roller coaster's hill
Where the bottom will drop out
And the worst year ever
Will be fondly remembered
As "the good old days"

August 15, 2020
Edmonds, Washington

I have no idea. I'm a poet, not a clairvoyant.

**My Recorded Existence**

My Instagram feed
Which once was a collection
Of flowers, pet photos,
And generally neat things
Lately has devolved
Into nothing but a wall
Of deep reddish oranges
And darkly rich navies
As the sunsets in this town
Have filled the frame
Of my recorded existence

August 15, 2020
Edmonds, Washington

**Into Winter's Eventual Embrace**

Even in the middle of summer
The signs are starting to show
That the season is waning
And that autumn is coming
The unstoppable swinging
From heating to cooling
As we find ourselves moving
Quickly across the months
Into winter's eventual embrace

August 21, 2020
Edmonds, Washington

## Starting Is A Place

Starting is a place
In time and space
Beginning in your mind
Before moving outward
Becoming an actual thing
Filling your life with purpose
Occupying all of your days
Growing in importance
Until reaching completion
And you are thankful for
Having made the journey
Having started in the first place

August 21, 2020
Edmonds, Washington

## The Mind Is A Busy Place

The mind is a busy place
Like a wide-eyed kitten
Leaping on everything
That catches its attention.
Learning to rein it in
Teaching it to calm down
And actually quieting,
Connecting fully with
The energy beyond
The physical bonds
Feeling the Universe
Expanding outward
In each and every direction,
Becoming the connection
The energetic intersection
Between this point here
Where you currently are,
And every bit of all eternity

August 21, 2020
Edmonds, Washington

I listened to "Transatlanticism" by Death Cab For Cutie and wrote.

I did not intend to have two poems in a row whose titles ended with "Place."

**Making The Time**

Making the time
Is the most important thing
Because that's the excuse
We most often throw out there
"I didn't have time…"
When the truth is
We honestly didn't choose
To spend our time to allow for that
Because we could have
If we had wanted to
I could have chosen to spend the evening
Sitting on the couch watching TV
But instead I wrote
And, when stitched together
With all of those other nights
When I also made the time
To write my thoughts down
I ended the year with a book
Over and over again
And now I've got a whole shelf
Filled with the books I wrote
The books that never
Would have been written
Had I not made the time
So, read back two poems
And get motivated
And get started
On that thing
You've always meant to do
You've always wanted to do
But never "had the time"
Start right now
Squeeze in fifteen minutes
To start
Do the same tomorrow
And continue
And keep it up

## August

Just a little
And then some more
Until you've reached your goal
And made your inner self proud
To have finally done that thing
You've always felt called to do
And in doing so
You've become a changed person
For the better
Becoming who you wanted to be
Who you were meant to be
Someone who Does Something Interesting

August 21, 2020
Edmonds, Washington

People tell me how they're impressed with how many books I've written, and they often say they've always meant to write a book, but never have. To them, I say, "Do it." Seriously. Anyone can do or become anything they want to be. They just need to have a desire and make the time.

Excuse me, I'm going to be an astronaut now.

**An Unadventurous Life**

An unadventurous life
Where everything is known
And nothing ever changes,
In an age where experience
And knowledge is available
And in easy reach to anyone
Extending their arm slightly,
Is the sentence condemned
To those who lack curiosity
To those who never leave
To those who never lust
For knowing what lies beyond
The comforts of the nest
Of the tree they've always flown to
When on autopilot returning home
From the automatically rote job
In the town that conveniently acts
As the singular defining answer
To all three words inadvertently
Encompassing this life:
Born, lived, died

August 21, 2020
Edmonds, Washington

I am so grateful and feel so lucky to have had the desire and drive to experience as much of the world in this life as possible. I sometimes wonder how things would have been different had I never left the town I grew up in.

**Soft Pastels**

Soft pastels
Smoothing the edges
Of the memories
Making them shinier,
Richer, better places
To return to
To remember
Than they actually were
Which is a trap
A terrible ruse
Made to ensnare you
Into spending time
Back there,
Where things are great
While completely
Forgetting the hard lines
And stark reality
Of how it actually was
Tricking you into stopping
The forward momentum
You had in this life
Causing the pause
Slowing you down
Making you waste
Your most valuable
Your most precious resource,
The one you can never
Ever get more of:
Time

August 21, 2020
Edmonds, Washington

My biggest issue with existence on this planet is how quickly time flies by. I will never get used to it.

## Changing Your Mind

Being open enough to
Changing your mind
On a subject
Once firmly set in stone
Causes cracks
Tearing through
The foundation
Upon which
Everything else
Is built and
Softens the ground
Relaxes the stance
Making other
Major worldview changes
Not only possible
But probable
And a whole lot easier

August 25, 2020
Edmonds, Washington

**Here You Are**

When considering
Every avenue open to you
In your youth
And every possible direction
You could have taken
When the idea of the future
Is based on the whims
Of a fool just starting out
When experience and wisdom
Are complete unknowns and
Are distantly foreign concepts
The impossible chance
That you took the lifepath
That led you to this moment
Jagged, forking, and sporadic
Through decades of choices,
Life events, missteps, and mishaps
Are staggering in the improbable
But yet, here you are, all the same
And I'm thankful that you're here

August 25, 2020
Edmonds, Washington

**The Job Of A Poet**

The job of a poet
Is one that's never done
When I'm awake
I'm observing
The missed opportunities
Of a society engrossed
But hardly aware
When I'm asleep
I'm dreaming
Deeply within the wonders
Of unlimited potentialities
The Universe holds –
All of it is collected,
Reviewed, and processed
Then painstakingly painted
Onto the canvas of your brain
Stirring your imagination
With evocative words
And carefully chosen phrases
Given as a gift
From me to you
Making this
The most rewarding,
And least paying,
Job I've ever had

August 28, 2020
Edmonds, Washington

**I Need A Break**

I need a break
From the horrible news
From the terrible people
Making the headlines
With their awful actions
And their hurtful words
As if they were
Working hard, trying,
Making this year
Even worse
Than it already was
As unbelievable
As that is to process

August 28, 2020
Edmonds, Washington

I wrote this while listening to "West Coast" by Lana Del Rey.

**Pivoting**

When feeling
Beaten down
Try pivoting
To something
New, positive
To something
Happy, joyful
To something
Filling full of
Gratitude and
Thankfulness
Changing you
From negative
Into a positive
Before you're
Even aware
It's happened

August 28, 2020
Edmonds, Washington

When the first three lines were roughly the same length, I decided to try and see if I could continue writing lines like that. I didn't want to because I felt it was too constricting, but if you don't challenge yourself from time to time, you'll never know what you can do.

**With Edges Rough And Fuzzy**

Crinkly
Crackling
With edges
Rough and fuzzy
Tickling the ears
With a wavy distortion
Hot and rippling
Flickering like fire
Setting you on edge
Leaving you unsettled
Alert
Betraying your feelings
With an empty warning
Preparing for anything
While also knowing
There's nothing there
At all

August 28, 2020
Edmonds, Washington

The song, "Human Behaviour" by Björk came on my playlist and my mind latched onto the unsettling distortion at the edges of the song and wrote this.

**Unintended Trip**

I'm not letting myself go there
The place where this sad song
Is trying to lead me
I'm not letting myself feel
The deep feelings of loss
That this song is singing me
Luring me onto the couch
Where it's comfortable
Sitting in a place
I know as safe
As the melodies
Ease my mind back
To the places
I don't want to do
The same ones
I don't ever re-live
If I can ever help it
The same ones
Now playing prominently
Over and over
In my mind
As the song
Longer than I remember
Ties me up in emotions
The echoing sustain
Throws me in a car
The slow drumbeats
Lock me in
The deep bass
Thumps the engine to life
And drives off
With my mind
Leaving my body
Unable to press *stop*
Or remove the headphones
As this unintended trip
Continues on

Until the phone's
Already low battery, dies

August 28, 2020
Edmonds, Washington

Most of the poems I wrote tonight were inspired by music. I wrote this while listening to, "So Much Work" by Pete Yorn, and "Tomorrow, Wendy" by Concrete Blonde.

**There's Always More**

Are there more?
There's always more.
How is that possible –
That the ideas
Just seem to flow
From nothing
But yet,
There they are
They're always there
Even when my
Ass hits the chair
With a vacant mind
The fingers
Always do their thing
And translate
The emotions
The pictures
The scenes
The ideas
That seemingly
Come from nowhere
By pressing patterns
On the keyboard
Making symbols
Lumped into groups
Holding meaning
Strung into lines
Forming notions
Building blocks
Conveying concepts
The whole process
To me is like
Making magic
Each and every time
I sit down to do this

August 28, 2020

August

Edmonds, Washington

Burn me as a witch because I'm making magic!

# SEPTEMBER

**To Know A Place**

I don't know why
My mind keeps returning
Back East, across the continent
Back to my hometown
The one I left
After graduating from high school
The one I've driven through
A handful of times since
The place where
Not a lot has changed
Except the people I knew
Who decided to remain
Are all much older
And that, really,
Is where my thoughts go
To the ones who stayed
Ventured out
And eventually returned,
And to the ones
Who never left
And I wonder why –
Was the allure
Of this wide world
Not enough?
Was the comfort of knowing
Nothing but his little sliver
Sufficiently able to satisfy
And stifle any curiosity
About what's Out There
Beyond the Berkshire hills?
But I have to remind myself
For some people, that *is* enough
To have the deep roots
To Know a place and its people
So thoroughly and completely
That you would never *ever* think
Of leaving your entire world

For an unknown
Because to them,
That’s a risky gamble
With little to no payoff
Other than loneliness
And unhappiness
In a world that’s already
Plenty scary enough

September 2, 2020
Edmonds, Washington

Every time I see one of the friend suggestions on Facebook that’s someone I went to school with and haven’t seen or thought of in 30 years, I think these thoughts – usually while I’m watching a vibrant sunset over the Olympic Mountains and Puget Sound while wondering, “With all of this in the world, why Dalton, Massachusetts?” I thought I would try and answer that from what I assume their perspective would be.

**Giving Balance**

A little bit of this
A little bit of that
In equal measure
Giving balance
To the evening
While still
Getting all
That I hoped for

September 2, 2020
Edmonds, Washington

**Left Swamped And Sinking**

Left swamped
And sinking
By likeminded
Devotees leaving
Those in trouble
To bail themselves out
After causing
The sinking
By going too fast
And making waves
Without thought
Or consideration
Because when
You're in a parade
Of people who don't care
About anyone else
Common courtesy
Is a rare commodity
In this real-life metaphor
For what they believe in

September 5, 2020
Edmonds, Washington

Not at all surprised by what happened at the Trump boat parade in Texas today.

**The Wrong Kind Of Gray**

This morning is lit by the
Wrong kind of gray
Still entirely too bright
To allow for the desired
Hunker-down do-nothing
Kind of day we planned
Maybe it's the clouds
Are they too thin
And letting through
Too much light?
Are they not dense enough
To do their job
Of blocking the sun?
Either way
This has an effect
That prevents the plans
That had been set
Back yesterday
When we saw the forecast
And knew what
We wanted to do
With this cloudy,
Sad Saturday

September 5, 2020
Edmonds, Washington

This is not true at all, but Kari did remark this morning that it was "the wrong kind of gray," outside.

**The Out-Of-Focus Photo**

The out-of-focus photo –
A sea of bright lights,
Colorful, soft, and blurry
Turning the night scene
Showing the panorama
Of this city as something
Ethereal, magical, otherworldly,
And completely desirable
A feeling of wanting,
Needing to be there in the frame
Captured perfectly in an image
That stops the scrolling
Of everyone, every time
Making them wish
They were here
In this enchanted place

September 5, 2020
Edmonds, Washington

Recently, I took a blurry picture of the art installation in Edmonds where lights were put into the street. Every time I look at my Instagram profile, that photo makes me pause and think how it looks like something you'd see in an ad, or an album cover, capturing a feeling rather than an object.

I wrote this while listening to "NYC" by J Lisk on repeat.

**The Need To Explore**

Sometimes
The need to explore
Becomes so much more
Than we are able to handle
So, we take off
To change the view
To something new
In hopes that it will
Tamp down that feeling
To something manageable
To prevent us from making
A rash decision always hiding
Just out of view, demanding
That we start planning
Something drastic
Like a move as a way
To fulfil the wanderlust
That has already ruined
So many opportunities
In so many places
Over so many years
Like a never-ending curse
That's stuck on repeat
Until this set of lives
On this planet are over

September 5, 2020
Edmonds, Washington

I wrote this while listening to Ryan Adams' cover of Taylor Swift's song, "Shake It Off."

**The Good Sleep**

Lately every night
Has been filled with
The good sleep
The kind where
I'm out instantly
And wake up
Eight solid hours later
Renewed and refreshed
Completely and utterly
Leaving me wondering
What's different now
From just last week
When the nights
Passed by so slowly

September 5, 2020
Edmonds, Washington

**The Line**

The line
Between
Being alive
And not
Is the difference
Of a fraction
Of a second
With one moment
You're here
And another
You're not
You're suddenly
Somewhere else
Instantly having
A new adventure
The shock of crossing
The line
Takes some time
To wrap yourself around
But after a while
You get used to it
And are happy
To be rid of the weight
The heaviness
The density
The weariness
That we're used to wearing
Here in this place
While feeling
The energy and the knowing
Resuming as if you'd never
Ever been gone
Because in a way
You haven't
You're just returning
To your normal state
And your normal place

## September

Between the lives
Between the plays
We act out
In our lives
The roles
We change
Like clothes
Each time
We come back

September 6, 2020
Edmonds, Washington

**The Little Snippets**

The little snippets
The tiny memories
That fill your body
With who you were
And where you're from
Only to make you
Who you are

September 6, 2020
Edmonds, Washington

**The Future Is Mine**

The past
Is remembered fondly
The present
Is lucky and amazing
The future
Is mine to fill completely
With the best I can dream

September 6, 2020
Edmonds, Washington

**The Parade Of The**

It's not so much poor planning
(Because there is none)
Or a distinct lack of editing
(Because there is plenty)
That has led me to this point
Where we are witness
To such an odd event
The parade of The
Where every poem
I've written lately
Has begun with "The"
I absolutely didn't plan it
As I just write what I feel
And I can't change it
Since I write them
Since I leave them
Done by date
And that's unchangeable
Like the laws of physics
So, I would like to take this time
To recognize this oversight
Created by coincidence
And happily move on
With the rest of the collection

September 6, 2020
Edmonds, Washington

**After The End**

How am I doing
In this life
Am I achieving my goals?
Have I been learning my life lessons?
Or, is it that I'm realistically
More than halfway through
This life, this experiment,
And I feel like I just woke up
Form an extended nap
That went decades too long
And I'm way behind
So far behind that I don't know
If I can catch up
With where
With what
With who
I'm supposed to be
Or what I'm meant to accomplish
I know in the end
It really doesn't *hugely* matter
Because it all starts again
Sometime later
But I'm here now
And I want to make the most
Of the dwindling time I have
To live big
And make a difference
To have this time around
Be one of substance
Would feel so great
When reviewing
How I did
After the end

September 6, 2020
Edmonds, Washington

More Life Between Lives thinking on my mind today.

On a completely unrelated note, I made a cover for this collection that I *really* like. Normally, at some point about halfway through the year, I make the cover. Over the five or six months from then, until I actually publish the collection, I will completely redesign the cover half a dozen times.

But this one, I like a lot and would be happy for it to stick. We'll see how long it lasts.

**After Eight**

Like those little after dinner mints
My grandparents used to have
Called "After Eight"
The sky is now dark by that time
Save for the dusky orange band
Draining into the horizon
Separating the dark water
From the navying sky
A far cry from a month ago
When it was sunny and blue
At the exact same time
A far cry from next month
When we're saying the same
About After Seven instead

September 6, 2020
Edmonds, Washington

Two poems ago I commented about using the word "The" to title eight poems in a row. Now, I inadvertently wrote two consecutive poems starting with "After."

Sigh.

## This Year Continues

This year continues
At an unstoppable pace
Determined to be
The most unforgettable,
Unforgivable, horrible
Year lived through
In modern times
And, knowing 2020
We haven't even seen
The worst of it yet

September 11, 2020
Edmonds, Washington

**The Verbal Touch**

The voice
The words
The timbre
The tone
The message
The meaning
The reception
The receiving
Add up
And play
The body
Like an instrument
Echoing
The sentiment
Stirring
The passion
Building
The emotion
Amplifying and
Reflecting
The energy
Back a thousand-fold
As the verbal touch,
Up until now only
Caressing the mind,
Becomes physical
Pouring forth
The impassioned song –
The two-part harmony
Of the duet's beauty

September 11, 2020
Edmonds, Washington

Written while listening to the instrumental version of The Cure's driving eight-minute song, "Disintegration."

**The Narrow Container**

Needing quiet
Exploring silence,
Space,
And everything
The vast emptiness contains
Once there
We grow to become
The expanded versions of ourselves
And can no longer fit
Into the narrow container
We once were

September 11, 2020
Edmonds, Washington

**What Lies Ahead**

Heart racing
As the ship
Is lancing
Through space
Not knowing
What lies ahead
Somewhere there
In the darkness
Only aware
Of the signal
Warning of
The danger
We're rushing into
Faster than light
Not knowing
What to expect
So, needing to be
Ready for anything
When we get there
To the station
Far beyond help
Or assistance
Just us, on our own
Doing what we do
When we get there
In three…
Two…
One…

September 11, 2020
Edmonds, Washington

It's been a very long time since I wrote a science-fiction poem and I thought I'd give it a shot.

**A Deliberate Thoughtfulness**

When treading through life
There must be
A deliberate thoughtfulness
That accompanies existence
Without it,
We're just selfish ogres
Thoughtlessly smashing through
The cosmic web binding us together
With it,
We're elevated beings
Carefully lifting others
Enhancing, enriching
Our shared experiences
And with it – humanity

September 11, 2020
Edmonds, Washington

**A Specific Flavor**

Sometimes I have an idea
That I'd like to fill this paper
With a specific savor
That matches the day
And what I'm feeling
But it doesn't always work like that
Like tonight when I was surprised
By the completely different flavor
Pouring from my creative source
Not what I had originally planned
But, despite the unintended surprise
I'm finding that it tastes even better
Leaving me at a distinctive place
I had never before anticipated

September 11, 2020
Edmonds, Washington

**Vibrancy**

The brightness of life
The vibrancy of it all
Appreciated fully
Every detail absorbed
Embraced tightly
Never letting go
Living every moment
Like an explosion of joy

September 11, 2020
Edmonds, Washington

**Steering Me Right**

In the moment
When things go wrong
Life feels confusing,
Terrible, and frustrating
But with enough distance,
Perspective, and wisdom
Is when I can clearly see
The Universe had Plans
And was steering me
Right where I needed to be

September 11, 2020
Edmonds, Washington

**Impact**

We all leave an impact
On people, places, and things
What is the underlying intention
Behind each action you make?
Positive or negative?
High energy or low?
What do you want your legacy,
The echoing waves of impact
Spreading out from your time
Spent in this life, to be?

September 11, 2020
Edmonds, Washington

**Particulates**

The tiny particulates
Too small to see
When viewed up close
Stack upon each other
In layer after layer
Across the distance
Obscuring the view
Slightly, at first
But then multiplying
Opaquing the sight
Making it impossible
To discern features
Farther out and away
Making everything
Blend into whiteness

September 11, 2020
Edmonds, Washington

The fires that are devastating the West Coast are all pretty far away from here, but it's still hanging thick in the air. I can't even see the water, which is only a mile away. It all just blends together with the sky due to all the smoke.

Auto-correct does not like the word, "opaquing."*

*I do.

**Overshadowed**

All of the good things
And amazing discoveries
This year has brought
Are all overshadowed,
Each and every one,
By the bigger calamities
That have befallen us
Nationally and globally
On a scale never seen

September 12, 2020
Edmonds, Washington

**Stepping Out**

After being cooped up inside
Sometimes I need a good
Stepping out
To change the scene
To see something new
To experience what's out there
Jut to know there's more to life
Than the walls surrounding me now

September 12, 2020
Edmonds, Washington

I love staying in, but every once in a while, I just need to get out and walk (or drive) around this town.

**Point Of View**

These days it's less
A "point of view"
And more like a
"Deeply rooted,
 completely unchangeable,
 unshakable belief
 that you're more than willing
 to kill another human being over
 if they dare to disagree
 or say anything about it
 that indicates they don't share
 the same extreme fanatical faith
 and hold it to the same degree
 that you obviously do
 despite the fact that it
 clearly contradicts
 your other professed beliefs."

September 12, 2020
Edmonds, Washington

Remember when most people were pretty normal, had open minds, and could bridge philosophical differences to find a happy middle ground?

**The Color Above**

The color above
High up in the atmosphere
Sets the tone
For everything
That goes on below
From the longing look
To the clasping grasp
Through the reflection
That inevitably comes
While staring at the sky
Wondering what's next
Until the cycle resets
And repeats again

September 19, 2020
Edmonds, Washington

**From The Place Of Zero**

Completely restarting
From the blank page
Can be daunting
Faced with the fear
Of absolutely nothing
And having to come up
With a brand new something
Each and every time
When opening
When starting
From the place of zero
Always hoping
Always praying
Inspiration comes to mind
Right when it's needed
And, thankfully,
That creative place
Never seems to fail
Always delivering
Always on time

September 19, 2020
Edmonds, Washington

**Willing To Break It Completely**

Imagine being
So prideful
So full of
Selfishness
Where "ratings"
And the act of
"Winning"
Means more
Than the country itself
Imagine, someone
Willing to act
Hypocritically
Willing to cheat
So greedily
Willing to destroy
A society
Willing to break it
Completely
Just to be the one
Wielding, retaining
Power
To hold
To gloat
Over all others

September 19, 2020
Edmonds, Washington

How did we end up in this dark timeline?

**American Re-Revolution**

We are weeks away
From the kind of
Uncontainable rage
With many tens of
Millions marching
Fire in the streets
Lives given up
Freely for the notion
Of actual liberty
In a never-before-seen
Generation changing
American re-revolution
Kind of way
The unplacatable kind
That our usual comforts
Of Internet, cable TV,
And rampant obesity
Cannot hope to contain

September 19, 2020
Edmonds, Washington

This is not going to end well for anyone.

**The Gentle Pitter Patter**

The gentle pitter patter
The light morning murmur
Of the gray-tinged weather
Giving passing cars
That extra dimension
The audible whisper
Letting you know
It's a rainy day out there

September 19, 2020
Edmonds, Washington

I needed to normalize things a bit after those last two poems. Gee whiz.

**Preordained**

From the woods
Up in the hills
Where it's always
Colder, snowier
A too-large destiny
In a too-small place
The type of personality
Thereby preordained
To eventually land
In the big city
With all of the expected
And magnetically unavoidable
Snares and trappings
Contained within
For a character like that
To avoid and resist
The pitfalls at every step
But the truest test
Is to see if they can overcome
The inclinations of a life
Lived on a grand scale
And learn to thrive
In the midst of normalcy

September 19, 2020
Edmonds, Washington

**Is There A Ghost**

Is there a ghost
Lurking out there
In the darkness
Waiting to scare
And frighten me?
Wanting to terrify
Me completely?

Yes, of course
But don't be
So full of yourself
I'm not waiting
For *you* specifically
Any human will do
And work just as nicely
So, boo!

September 19, 2020
Edmonds, Washington

A tree by our door is dropping very bright red leaves, so I guess it's putting me in the autumn/Halloweeny mood.

**Building This Thing**

Building this thing
Word by word
Poem by poem
Page by page
Book by book
Is a fascinating way
To pass this life
Thank you
For reading along

September 19, 2020
Edmonds, Washington

Seriously, thank you. I really appreciate you.

**Into The Skip-Beat**

Stuck in the loop
Of creativity
My mind blank
The music playing
Through my headphones
Moving me
My fingers
Along
As the feelings swirl
And the words flow
Magically out onto
The page and through
The time between
Into the ink printed and
Delivered by the light
To your eyes
Touching your soul
Hopefully
In the right way
That resonates
And communicates
My love for this life
Into the skip-beat
Of your heart

September 19, 2020
Edmonds, Washington

**A Greater Whole**

The connection
To the above
Is the bridge
Of knowing
Pushing feeling
The impulses
That move us
In the right way
Pushing us
In the right direction
Toward the things
Meant to grow us
Into a greater whole

September 19, 2020
Edmonds, Washington

I've written nine poems tonight. I don't know why I haven't yet remembered what today's date is. Every time, I've had to glance at the dock which shows my iCal icon (and the date).

**Not Ready To Waive**

Pulling yourself out of the moment
Is such a difficult thing
When you're riding the wave
And you're not ready to waive
Goodbye to the feeling
You're hooked so completely into

September 19, 2020
Edmonds, Washington

I've been listening to Mount Dreams's song, "Home" on repeat for the last four poems. Such an amazing song.

**The Ones That Missed**

In what kind of world
Does this make sense
Where the ones that missed
And stuck in a neighbor's wall
Are held in higher regard
On the scale of trouble
Than the ones that killed her
Which aren't even considered
Which aren't even valued
Like the life they took
In the eyes of the law
And those in charge

September 24, 2020
Edmonds, Washington

About the murder of Breonna Taylor.

For some reason every day seems worse than the last.

## Not Blind

Justice is clearly not blind
Because all it sees is color
In order to determine fate
In matters of life and death

September 24, 2020
Edmonds, Washington

**Reviewing A Checklist**

The air matches the calendar
Rolling over into autumn
Just as the temperature dropped
Along with the leaves
Almost on cue
As if it were expected
Purely out of obligation
Like nature is just
Reviewing a checklist
And crossing things off
Or else the boss will get mad

September 24, 2020
Edmonds, Washington

**Obligation Is The Road**

Obligation is the road
No one wants to be on
Because there is no scenery,
No enjoyment, and no exits –
Just forward motion
At a crawling pace
In a car with no radio

September 24, 2020
Edmonds, Washington

**Brevity**

Brevity is often derided
For being lacking in content
As more pages
Only equals
Bigly intelligent
By the small minds
Who think bigger is better
And flashier is heartier
In each and every case
But more pages
Does not equal
A greater intellect
On the part
Of the author
Or the reader
It only looks
More impressive
On the shelf

September 24, 2020
Edmonds, Washington

My last few poems were much shorter than what I normally write, so I wrote this to make myself feel better about it.

**Interruption**

Waiting for the interruption
That inevitable derailment
That will stop the creativity
From continuing…
And, there it is. Sorry.

September 24, 2020
Edmonds, Washington

**The Pervasive Chill**

The thermometer says a number
Which is fine, normal, and good
But the pervasive chill in the air
Speaks entire volumes
Of what's coming this way
Sliding in over the next few weeks
Intending to barge in and sit firmly
Squashing any remaining plans
We had for anything outdoors
While also extinguishing the light
Ensuring we get the message
That it's time to hibernate

September 26, 2020
Edmonds, Washington

**West Coasting**

West coasting
Is a different way
Of acting, being,
Responding, and
Even spending time
Different priorities
Different feelings
Different outcomes
Freewheeling,
Gliding, breezing
In a way not found
On the other seaboard
As the Atlantic is aged
And ages those it touches
Unlike the Pacific
Younger, accessible,
And more relaxed –
Swelling with potential
In a way unknown
In the old place

September 29, 2020
Edmonds, Washington

**Like Bokeh In My Body**

Feeling like bokeh in my body
Softening, out of focus, and fuzzy
Home to so many variations
Wondering what is normalcy
At the same time deeply
Knowing I no longer care
Embracing the bubbly
Effervescent feeling
Swelling me up, up, up
Telling me to go with it
Letting loose completely
In the absolute certainty
Life is meant to be lived
Exactly like this
Always

September 29, 2020
Edmonds, Washington

Yesterday, Kari said the phrase, "like bokeh in my body," and, to her chagrin, I wrote it down immediately.

**Freedom To Be A Jumble**

Freedom to be a jumble
To not be perfectly even
To have rough-hewn edges
The kind that leave slivers
Deep under your skin
With each jarring impact
To be brash and loud
Instead of kind and quiet
Like we're expected to be
By a society that demands
Absolutely conformity
And placation with emotions
Violating their very nature
With their true definition
To be loose and liberated
In actions and mindset
In a nation that frowns
On any outward expression
Especially the truest kind
As we are conditioned
To always hold it all in
Every moment of every day
A perfectly complete picture
Instead of the jumble of pieces
We're actually made out of
That sometimes just wants
To be a messy heap
In the puzzle box

September 29, 2020
Edmonds, Washington

"Freedom to be a jumble," is another Kari quote from yesterday that I wrote down and said I would make into something.

## Society Has Devolved

Society has devolved
To the point where those
We most expect to be
Professional and
Presidential
Turns what should be
A presentation of ideas
A discussion of policy
Into an elementary school fracas
Complete with bullying,
Threats, and name calling

September 29, 2020
Edmonds, Washington

**Left For The Day**

How can it possibly be
That it's only just seven
And the sun
Has already left for the day
And the night
Has apparently punched in early
Greatly and seasonally
Changing the dynamics
Of my after-work time

September 30, 2020
Edmonds, Washington

**More Pictures**

I wish that
When I was younger
I had taken more pictures
Of myself
And had put myself
Prominently into the frame
More often
Instead of being so camera-shy
Ducking, and hiding
Every time someone said "Cheese"
So I could see that, at one time,
I not only possessed youth
But defined it
To see countless pictures
Of myself, every one
With my innocent eyes
And that always present
Wide, happy, hopeful smile
That were eventually
Ironed out by experience
And the passage of time

September 30, 2020
Edmonds, Washington

And I'm certain in twenty or thirty years I'll be saying the exact same thing about me right now in my forties.

September

# OCTOBER

**Shedding Skin**

Shedding skin
Removing the self
That no longer serves
What you want to become
Planning the plumage
Expressing the self
That is who you are
And where you are going
All for changing, swapping
The past version
For the future
Now in the present

October 3, 2020
Edmonds, Washington

Inspired by my monthly tarot reading by Onyx Healing on YouTube.

**Unsurprising**

In the midst of a global pandemic
It's unsurprising that the population segment
Who eschewed doctor's orders
To take the most basic of precautions
Are the ones who are beyond shocked
When they, and their loved ones
Fall ill with the contagious disease
And each and every one of them
Give their deathbed confession
Expressing regret for not wearing
The mask that could have saved them

October 3, 2020
Edmonds, Washington

Because perceived "freedoms" are apparently more important than breathing – or living.

## The Heap Of Thoughts

The ideas pile up
On the heap of thoughts
That have been
Fully reviewed
Over and over
That have gone
Unacted on
Despite the gut
Loudly telling
Actively demanding
Action on this,
The better judgement
That's been ignored
For much too long

October 3, 2020
Edmonds, Washington

**Muting The Moon**

The light
Diffuse
The clouds
Thick
Like a spill
Of dirty cotton candy
Obscuring the stars
Muting the moon
Setting the tone
Amid the darkness
And shadows
Down below
Surrounding
Enveloping
The night
Setting the stage
Of what's to come
Later tonight

October 3, 2020
Edmonds, Washington

Now we're in October, things are inadvertently spoooooky.

## Quantum Entanglement

Quantum entanglement,
The energy binding all things
Extends across time and space
Connecting you to everything
From the past as well as
What's still to come
Like a lifeline attached
To the future version
You will soon become
Guiding, pulling you
Or, sometimes it feels like
It's actually dragging you along
Feeling every bump and scrape
Teaching you valuable life lessons
Along your route this time around
Because you can never learn
Experiencing only perfection
And nothing here is coincidence
But you will still end up
Exactly where you need to be
Because that's how this works
The right place, at the right time
Always.

October 3, 2020
Edmonds, Washington

**Distillation**

The mind takes thoughts
And puts them through
A deeply repeated
Distillation process
Breaking down
Each moment
Reviewing, replaying,
Crushing, pressuring,
Regretting, wishing
Things had been different
In small and large ways
So hopefully
The next time
The outcome will be
Different
And more in line
With what's desired

October 3, 2020
Edmonds, Washington

**Go With The Flow**

Go with the flow
To see where it goes
Because you can't always
Be a rock, unmoving, unyielding
Since that's how you get
Submerged, buried, forgotten
Or, worse yet to the inflexible,
Still bowled over by the river
Knocked over, tossed aside,
Indistinguishable from the debris
When the intensity ramps up
Instead of being miles away
Having trusted the universe
And ended up in a better place

October 3, 2020
Edmonds, Washington

**Woodstove**

Someone somewhere
Has their woodstove
Burning so sweetly
Providing them warmth
Giving me memories

October 3, 2020
Edmonds, Washington

**Burning Brightly**

It's better to be
Burning brightly
And having lived
A remarkable life
Rich with wisdom,
Full of experiences,
And having touched
So many in the process
Than the opposite –
Empty and boring,
Poorly experienced,
And quickly forgotten

October 3, 2020
Edmonds, Washington

**Feeling The Light**

Feeling the light
Shining in the mind's eye
Warming me inside
Filling me with completion
Resting me assured
Of the strange direction
This road has taken me
That this is where
I am supposed to be

October 3, 2020
Edmonds, Washington

Written while listening to "Taillights Fade" by Buffalo Tom.

**Remember Back**

The ability to remember back
Twenty, thirty years
Is something that makes me uneasy
That I am old enough
To think back *decades*
That I am old enough
To be the parent of an adult
A person whose actual age
Is what I feel like I am inside
Instead of being this older shell
Clearly showing its wear and tear
Of having traveled
More than halfway through
This body's journey…
Assuming I'm lucky, that is

October 3, 2020
Edmonds, Washington

The song, "Taxi Ride" by Tori Amos came onto my Spotify playlist. I remember in the very early 2000s when this song came out and how I found her journey around the country, writing about her experiences, to be a source of inspiration. Now, I just think how it's been nearly twenty years since I first heard it.

I've said it before, and I will keep saying it: I really have such a huge problem adjusting to the flow of time here. A slow and heavily dense world where time whizzes by like lightning.

**Earth Is**

Earth is
So thick, and dense
Heavy beyond compare
Weighted down
By emotions
And mental heft
Such a tired place
Filled with challenges
And barbaric violence

Earth is
So bright, and happy
Filled with fascination,
Beauty beyond compare,
And delight anywhere
You choose to find it

Earth is
Such an absolutely
Confounding and conflicting place
Filled with amazing contrasts
Such opportunity for learning
And ability to experience so much –
Which is exactly why we're here

October 3, 2020
Edmonds, Washington

**Continuing With Ease**

A week, a year,
A decade, or two
It doesn't matter
Exactly how long
Since I've written –
Things like this
Are picked up
Instantly, immediately
Continuing with ease
Completely without effort
Resuming my creativity
As if no time has passed
From then until now
Because the well, the Source,
Is still fully connected
And is still providing
Everything I need

October 10, 2020
Edmonds, Washington

Okay, I'm being a little dramatic here – it's only been one week since I've written any poems.

**The Muddle Of Us**

The liquid that we are
Pouring, mixing,
Clouding, becoming
Something greater
The muddle of us
Puddling together
Appreciating detailing
All there is to know
About each another
Intimately connecting
Understanding everything
As only our fluidic selves can
Beyond this physical space

October 10, 2020
Edmonds, Washington

**Making News In The Present**

A fire in the place of the past
Making news in the present
Barging in and making itself
A part of my modern world
Terribly, in a way I don't want
To think of that memory-laden place
Now associating it with the mire
And the stain of this abysmal year
Reaching out and slapping the past
Associating it with modern hate
Infecting it in the eyes of the world
Taking the good things I knew
Carelessly tossing them on the fire
Charring them beyond recognition

October 10, 2020
Edmonds, Washington

My hometown of Dalton, Massachusetts made the national news this weekend. A farmer stacked his huge, wrapped haybales and painted a pro-Biden message on them. Someone took offense to it and torched the whole thing. At least they caught the guy, but now that farmer's animals are without food for the winter. I really can't believe how people are acting.

**A Blurring Montage**

The contrasts here are so intense
A slow and heavily dense world
Where time whizzes by frighteningly fast
Middle-aged and I still can't get my bearings
Spun around by the speed of it all
Morning, daytime, sunset, and darkness
Flashing by in a blurring montage
Like a looping television show cut scene
Endlessly stuck on fast-forward
Until when it abruptly doesn't
That moment of pause and reflection
When time finally no longer matters
And I have a chance to take a breath
And appreciate the run I've had

October 10, 2020
Edmonds, Washington

**Cautious Times For The Nimble**

These are indeed
Cautious times
For the nimble
Outnumbered
By the heavy –
Holding hammers
And looking to do
That one thing
They know

October 10, 2020
Edmonds, Washington

I wrote a note on my phone that said, "The cautious times of the Nimble." When this odd phrase popped into my head, I assumed it would evolve into some sort of a short story (it still might). When going over my notes, just now, I saw it and thought I would at least try to see what I could do with it. Short, but accurate.

**Beauty**

Don't ever
Lose sight
Of the beauty
Without that
Appreciation
We are blind
As a species

October 10, 2020
Edmonds, Washington

There is so much pain and suffering on this planet, but there is also SO MUCH beauty. Don't ever lose sight of the beauty.

**The Twinkle Lights In My Periphery**

The twinkle lights in my periphery
Act equally as such a gentle,
And actively energetic, reminder
Of the home beyond this place
Where we are on loan from
Where we will return to
When we reach our due dates
Happier and lighter
Amidst the pure joy
Never experienced here

October 10, 2020
Edmonds, Washington

**Repeatedly**

Confined closely
Trapped together
Wrapped tightly
By choice.
Confidently
Breathlessly
Repeatedly

October 10, 2020
Edmonds, Washington

**Just Start**

To the middle-aged mother
Who wants to create
But feels it's too late
To make a difference,
Just start.
To the elderly man
Who thinks it's futile
To do anything
Because life is over,
Just start.
To the person
Who has an idea
But doesn't know
Where to begin,
Just start.
My goodness
Just start
Anywhere
And figure it out
Along the way
Is infinitely better
Than doing nothing
And living with regret
Wishing you had
Just started back then

October 17, 2020
Edmonds, Washington

Successful creatives say it again and again: just start.

**Live Deftly**

The weight of the past
Shrugged off
Releases the burden
Alleviates the encumbrance
Frees the self
To be fully present
For the present
To live deftly
Ready to catch
Any and all opportunities
Throwing themselves
In your direction

October 17, 2020
Edmonds, Washington

**Diet Of Fear**

Cognizant of the changes
Currently underway
The uprising of voices
The upswelling of support
For a different world
For lasting change
Based on hope
Instead of the diet of fear
They've been feeding us
As the only option to eat
Which we woke to reject
Now knowing we can choose
A future free of dystopia –
One focused on cooperation
And mutual respect
One where we no longer
Have to always be afraid
Never again knowing
Hatred's continual beratement
From the very top on down
Because who wants to live like that

October 17, 2020
Edmonds, Washington

**New**

New
Is exciting
New
Is exhilarating
Is motivating
The experience
To experience
More
Is moving
To create
More
Always more
Uplifting and
Inspiring
To continue
Seeking out
More
Always more
Rewarding
And enriching
Those who choose
To seek out
What's new

October 17, 2020
Edmonds, Washington

Written while listening to "There Is A Light That Never Goes Out" by the Dum Dum Girls (cover of The Smiths's song).

**A New Wavelength**

Standing feeling
The energy of us
Rippling through
My heart, my being
Clearly knowing
This is the present
That was meant to be
Accomplishing all
The life goals we
Had set for this life
Never easy, but
Here we are
You and I
Getting it done
Checking things off
Rising up
Changing, becoming
A new wavelength
More intense
Setting us up
For interesting lives
In the future

October 17, 2020
Edmonds, Washington

Listened to "Standing In This Dream" by My Dear and just wrote.

## From Elsewhere Beyond

Upswelling within
That building sensation
Giving the knowing
That I'm on the right path
The gut instinct guiding
From elsewhere beyond
Leading me to pre-planned
Places and situations
Intended to provide experience
Designed to upgrade my soul
In this challenging world
Chosen like a crucible
To distill the best in us
To foster proficiencies
The kind you can't get
Incarnating elsewhere

October 17, 2020
Edmonds, Washington

A few Life Between Lives, soul world-inspired, poems tonight.

**Caught Between Placements**

Sidestepping the slimming
Caught between placements
Finding the resulting ending
To be one that's not wanted
But still serves the intention
Despite the best inclination
Leading onward years later

October 17, 2020
Edmonds, Washington

Listening to "Inside" by Toad The Wet Sprocket and writing nonsensical phrases while trying to keep them the same length.

**Creation**

Creation
Is the highest
Most pure expression
You can achieve
Taking your talents
And your ideas
And making something
Tangible out of them
Allowing you to express
Your feelings
In a way that changes
In a way that leaves
The experiencer
Changed as a result
Hopefully, in a way
That inspires them
To reach within
And share in the
Gift of creation
Leaving a positive mark
On society, in this place,
In this time, we live in

October 17, 2020
Edmonds Washington

I know so many people who are creatives, who feel called to express themselves through art, through writing, through so many varied ways. It's amazing.

**Writing Is Like Meditation**

Writing is like mediation
When you close your eyes
And get caught up in the feeling
Not worried about anything
But expressing yourself
Through your words
The patterns on the keyboard
Forming the words and phrases
Expressing the concepts and ideas
Just feeling and expressing
Pouring out from deep within
A joy of manifestation
Feeling the energy
Through the flowing
Of thoughts
From the Source
Through me
Into the book
Like the trapping
Of potential energy
Waiting for the pages
To be opened and read
Tapping into the energy
Connecting me to you

October 17, 2020
Edmonds, Washington

I had "Strange Condition (Rock Version)" by Pete Yorn on repeat while writing this with my eyes closed and feeling energy radiation from me like a very hot lightbulb…like a heat lamp bulb – the kind you used to find at not great motels in the eighties, which seemed kind of fancy, but they really weren't.

That's a terrible analogy.

**Nature's Delicate Touch**

A bright patch of green
Growing, glowing brightly
Deeply in the grooves
Of the manhole cover
The mossy crayon
Leaving its mark
Livening up the street
In such a small, subtle way
But still so noticeable
Making me appreciate
Nature's delicate touch

October 17, 2020
Edmonds, Washington

A (mostly) true story. It was actually a Verizon panel in the sidewalk.

**Knowing The Joy**

The time that elapsed
From the moment
I opened the mailbox
To defiantly sliding
The completed ballot
Into the ballot box
Outside the library
Two miles away
Was under thirty minutes
The whole process
From opening
To reading
To researching
To filling out
To re-packaging
To driving
To submitting
Everything done
In under half an hour
Knowing the joy
The others have felt
Having done their duty
To save this country

October 17, 2020
Edmonds, Washington

When we were dropping off our ballots, there was about a dozen other people who had done the exact same thing. Many were taking photos of their ballots being slid into the box. They were all giddy with joy.

**Instant Ballotification**

When I saw it sitting there
In my mailbox it felt like
My chance to change things
Had finally arrived
Like I had the power
To exercise the reversal
Of my frustrations
To fix this fucked-up world
By taking my pen
Filling in a bubble
And sending it off
Like I was dumping bleach
On a stubborn patch of mold
Killing it, removing it,
Cleaning up this place
Giving me that
Instant ballotification
I've been craving
So very deeply
For the past four years

October 17, 2020
Edmonds, Washington

I would like the world to evolve to a more compassionate and happier place.

**The Outcome**

The outcome of the next few weeks
Is completely unknown for me
But, by the time this is read
You will know how it all ended
Having the knowledge
Being on the other side
Of the sea of uncertainty
Separating me from you
The past here
To the future there

October 22, 2020
Edmonds, Washington

Note from January 9, 2021: Gee whiz, what an utter and complete emotional slog it's been from when this was written until now.

**Bypassing The Full Fall Crispness**

The cold outside
Feels like a betrayal
Feels like nature
Became bored
With how things are
And skipped ahead
A full month
Bypassing
The full fall
Crispness
I have come to expect
I have waited a year for
Plunging us gravy-deep
Into the season of Thanksgiving

October 22, 2020
Edmonds, Washington

**The Humming**

The humming in the ear
Is signaling the start
When the words heard are
Meaning less than those
We have found from
Reading from the pages
Between the understanding
Beginning this new place

October 22, 2020
Edmonds, Washington

I don't know what this means. It started from hearing the long humming guitar distortion from the end of the live version of the song, "Godless" by The Dandy Warhols which made me write the first line, and then I just went from there.

**This Year Is Exhausting Me**

This year is exhausting me
On each and every front
Like I'm standing stuck
In the center of a rotary
Seeing nothing but
Angry traffic blurring by
All of it honking constantly
With their high beams on
While tossing trash at me
In an endlessly speeding parade
Never ever letting up
And every little while
The curb recedes just a bit
Letting the traffic encroach
On my space, slightly closer
Making me feel unsafe
And a little more afraid
Until I can do nothing else
But take my chances
And make a break for it
In this nightmare place
Where it is guaranteed
That no one will brake

October 22, 2020
Edmonds, Washington

## Placement

What to do when
How to ensure
The best placement
When deciding
How to pursue dreams
Which goals are closer
To being able to achieve
And of those,
Which have the potential
For the greatest return
In this weighty judgement
That I've never cared for
But I seem to be always doing

October 22, 2020
Edmonds, Washington

**The Last Lamp Run Down**

The last ramp run down
Exiting the freeway
Still going at highway speed
Careening around the corner
Too fast for comfort
Two wheels lifting off the ground
Just for a moment
Just as a warning
Of the danger to come
To the occupants
Not wearing seatbelts
Finding them too restrictive
Cheering on the whole process
Not caring about the peril
Unaware of the potential
Dead ending rapidly approaching
Only caring about themselves
And not the innocent
Accidentally
Fatefully
Ending up in their way
Not even worth
A touch to the brakes
But still
The ones who knew
The offenders
Would forever
Describe this moment
As a "tragic" incident
And not the result
Of terrible people
Causing harm
With their thoughtless actions
Because no matter the crime
Everyone is painted as a saint
When they're gone

October 24, 2020
Edmonds, Washington

Not inspired by anything, other than I wanted to re-frame anti-maskers in a different light. I had only written down the title phrase and imagined this scene and wrote about it.

**The Echoing Delay**

The echoing delay
Centered around
The latent desires
Leading me away
To what I found
Realizing my wishes

October 24, 2020
Edmonds, Washington

Lately, I've been taking a more zen-like approach to writing, by turning on my Poetry mix on Spotify and writing whatever I feel based on the song that comes on. I wrote this to "Anybody Wanna Take Me Home" by Ryan Adams.

**Mute The News**

Sometimes the need
To just mute the news
To block out the sound
Of the human cacophony
And retreat to solitude
Running away to the woods
In order to breathe deeply
Filling so absolutely and
Completely full of the
Intoxicatingly-needed
Comfortingly-restoring
Embrace of nature
Nurturing, refurbishing,
Fixing what society broke
So deep within me
Making me feel whole again
Giving me the strength
To once again dip back
Into the toxic fray
That every one of us is
Submerged and subjected to
Each and every day

October 24, 2020
Edmonds, Washington

The news gets so overbearing and weighty, that sometimes I reach a point where I have to tell Kari to stop reading me articles or headlines.

"The Sun" by The Naked And Famous is such an amazing song to write to on repeat.

**Some Moments**

Moments sometimes flow effortlessly
To where you don't even notice
The passage of time
Because it is like a sweet dessert
Or an enjoyable song
That you just want over and over
But that's not always the case
As some moments
Are jarring like a rumble strip
Where one second
Is crudely stapled
To another second
Each moment
Is a painful slog
Tripping, falling,
Crawling over nails
For what feels like miles
Terrible seconds
Strung together
So slowly - decades away
From reaching a minute
All the while knowing
You have hours upon hours
Of this to get through

October 24, 2020
Edmonds, Washington

Yikes!

**My First Interaction With A Driverless Car**

My first interaction
With a driverless car
Was nearly a disaster
In the CVS parking lot
As I was backing up
And three-quarters out
Of my parking spot
When from my right
Came a white blur
Clearly not stopping
Causing me to slam
Hard on my brakes
And I stared in disbelief
As the Tesla driving by
Was completely empty –
Devoid of any humans
Because the car's owner
Was standing on the curb
Giving me a waive
That said both, "Sorry!"
And "Don't worry!"
Like he was trying
To reassure me that
Everything was fine
As he got into his car
And it drove away
Leaving me wondering
Who was in charge
And making me more
Than a little afraid
For the coming years

October 24, 2020
Edmonds, Washington

True story. This past week I got my flu shot at CVS and this happened when I was trying to leave.

**Only You Do**

Stifling your creativity
Denying your talents
Preventing the person
From becoming the one
Who yearns to grow
So, please trust your gut
And express yourself
Exactly how you feel
Even if no one agrees
Or understands, it's okay
They don't need to –
Only *you* do

October 25, 2020
Edmonds, Washington

**Feeling The Connection**

Meditating –
Closing eyes
Feeling the
Connection
Across time
And space
To the place
Where I feel
Most at home
Where total joy
And buoyancy
Are the air
We breathe
And love is the
Temperature
That surrounds
And permeates
Every aspect
Of everything
And the uplifting
The light-filled
Total uplifting
Of that connection
You can go to
Anytime you want
Just press pause
On this world
For a short time
And enjoy that one
As deeply
And wholly
As you desire

October 25, 2020
Edmonds, Washington

It's been an embarrassingly long time since I've meditated, so as I was sitting at my desk, I wondered if I could close my eyes, quiet my mind, and meditate while writing. It turns out, I could.

Written while listening to "You And I" by Washed Out.

**Every Moment You Choose**

Continuing into the delving
Started from the previous
Moment
Continuing the thought
Created a few minutes before
Like stepping into a dream
At the exact moment you left
But with full awareness
And complete control
To live that other life
In that other place
The one between
Here and there
Letting the energy
Dance and swirl
Like otters playing
The light radiating
The heat warming
Giving this one second
The glowing
And the feeling
That perfection
Is found within
Every moment
You choose

October 25, 2020
Edmonds, Washington

A continuation of the last poem.

**Millions Of Superheroes**

The feeling
Building
The momentum
Rolling
Across the country
As ordinary people
Tired of all the shit
Finally take a stand
And make their voices heard
Millions of superheroes
Braving standing for hours in the rain
Continuing despite intimidation
Overcoming all the obstacles
Persisting through the setbacks
All thrown to block, delay, prevent
But each and every time
They stood up to the threat
And made their voice heard
Loud and clear
That they will not be threatened
That they will not be intimidated
They will not be silenced
And that we will take back
This country which is for
ALL people
No matter your beliefs
No matter where you're from
No matter your color
No matter where you live
No matter who you love
ALL people

October 25, 2020
Edmonds, Washington

**Reaching Out**

Reaching out
Holding onto
The feeling
The knowing
That's holding
Onto me back
Reciprocating
And reflecting
Every bit of it
In an endless
Circle, looping
Until we end up
Colliding and
Collapsing
Under the weight
Of our spiraling
Gravitational pull

October 31, 2020
Edmonds, Washington

**The Invisible Killer**

The spooky day
Made even scarier
By the invisible killer
Stalking every one of us
Wanting to infest and infect
Because a pain in your chest
Is a now a certain sign of death
Cancelling all our normal plans
Preventing us from going out
Keeping us huddling at home
Making us afraid to see others
Crippling us with fear
And making us run away
Every time someone coughs
And a sneeze clears the room
Making everyone wonder
Not if, but when will they get it

October 31, 2020
Edmonds, Washington

**The Summer I Misplaced**

Despite how awful this year has been
It is also flying by faster than any before
Making me wonder what happened
To the summer I misplaced
The one I had so many plans for
And now I'm teetering
On the edge of November
Indicating that this year
Is thankfully, nearly over
But I can't help but feel
That I've slept walked
For the past eight months
And now I'm groggily awake
Wondering what the hell happened
Hoping this was just a nightmare
But also knowing, that yes, it is
Something I actually lived through
Instead of having slept through

October 31, 2020
Edmonds, Washington

## The Universe Is Guiding

When something you want
Is knocked out of your hands
And you are soundly rejected
Instead of feeling dejected
Be happy in the knowing
That The Universe is guiding
You away from what isn't serving
Your best interests, and is steering
You towards your true path
Even if it's not the road
You had intended walking on

October 31, 2020
Edmonds, Washington

**Forward Is The Only Direction**

Sometimes you have to just keep going
Even when you lose that thing
That's most important to you
Leaving it under the pile of pages
Falling from the calendar
Forming sedimentary layers
Burying it firmly in the past
At least you know where it is
And later, when you're done,
You can go back and visit
But for now, you have to keep pushing
You have to keep going
Because forward
Is the only direction
We have available to us

October 31, 2020
Edmonds, Washington

**Unproven**

Seeing is believing but
“Knowing” isn’t proving
Unless it’s been peer-reviewed
Until then, it’s unproven

October 31, 2020
Edmonds, Washington

**Pinballing Through Life**

Pinballing through life
Bouncing randomly
Hitting the walls, hard
Being slapped by the paddles
Racking up points despite
Lacking any clear plans
Until finally
Slipping through the gate
Getting a moment to pause before
Being shot back into the game
Repeating the process once again
Playing the role over and over
On the machine with unlimited games
With the player who has unlimited time

October 31, 2020
Edmonds, Washington

## Complexing The Identity

More than buoyant
Because that still implies
You're mired in the water
Attached to the density
When in reality
Being ethereal
Is a better descriptor
Lighter than air
Free from gravity
Being part of the Above
Not just feeling the energy
But being the energy
And its various forms
Complexing the identity
Of how I view myself
As a vaporous ribbon of light
Beyond the reach of negativity
Choosing to bask in the glory
Of the happiness that abounds
And is found deeply within

October 31, 2020
Edmonds, Washington

## Like Watching Old Episodes

Seeing old photos of yourself
Is like watching old episodes
Of a long-running TV show
From more than a decade ago
Where the screen is square
The resolution is grainy
The color is terribly faded
And the technology is dated
Yes, the actors are younger
But they're also dumber
Lacking the experience
They've since gathered
In the ensuing years
And it seems silly
This was even allowed
To be on the air
To occupy such precious time
And somehow it managed
To hang on, season after season,
But it did
And each time, it improved
Becoming better
Becoming the version of you
You find yourself in today

October 31, 2020
Edmonds, Washington

# NOVEMBER

**Waiting Is The Hardest Part**

Waiting is the hardest part
For the outcome
You chose
For the conclusion
You hoped for
As it drags on
For what feels like
Entirely too long
While trying to ignore
The swirling conspiracies
And the countless schemes
From those who wanted
And tirelessly worked for
The opposite result
As the whole country
Unbalanced, unstable,
Top-heavy, and angry
Teeters on the razor
Making right now
A hard place to be

November 7, 2020
Edmonds, Washington

**The Cliffhanger Conclusion**

Why did we expect
The compulsive liar
To change his song
When it all reached
The cliffhanger conclusion
This intensely fragile summation
Where the system is most delicate
And he's frantically trying
To light match after match
Throwing them with intention
On the flammable mixture
Carefully cultivated to explode
And it absolutely would
If it weren't for the steady wind
Growing and blowing out
Each flame of hatred
As they're sparked
Keeping the detestation
Firmly at bay
With an air of reason
And calm that's been sorely missed

November 7, 2020
Edmonds, Washington

**Submerged**

The grossly heavy intensity
Waterlogging this week
Weighing down each moment
Wondering what's the outcome
Of that big thing we did on Tuesday
While slogging through our days
Watching the world hold its breath
And wishing for this damnable year
To finally give us all a break
From the absolute insanity
It's had us submerged in

November 7, 2020
Edmonds, Washington

**Nightlight Of Hope**

The calendar says the year is nearly over
But, by now, we all know better
That the remaining weeks
Will continue to assail us
And will feel like months
But we've been given a glimmer,
A faint nightlight of hope
Shining in the distance
And, for now, that's all we need –
A direction to head toward
And something to focus on

November 7, 2020
Edmonds, Washington

I wrote these in the morning before I knew that Biden had won the election.

**Completely Unaware**

An unexpected mountain of hope
Was delivered this morning
Catching us completely unaware
Because hope has been something
We've learned to not plan for

November 7, 2020
Edmonds, Washington

Written at night, after a day of joy.

**Pushed Past Normalcy**

Reading the news
And feeling the feeling
Building, beaming,
Absolutely *shining*
Filling the entire room
With a halo of radiance
That we now have a chance
To halt the regression
The turn back the hate
To push past normalcy
And maybe enter a time
When we actually cared
About other people
And helped elevate
*Everyone* instead of the "ME"
We've known lately

November 7, 2020
Edmonds, Washington

## A Lingering Flash

Each memorable note
Brings me through time
Fully back there
To a lingering flash
Even more familiar
Than the notes themselves
Where the edges are blurred,
Dark, and haunted,
With sepia-toned ghosts
That never end up aging
Swirling around the periphery
Dancing, enjoying the moment
Knowing it's one
That'll be revisited often
Every time I hear this song
Which seems to come up
With a regular frequency
On my Spotify playlists
As if planned by the spirits

November 7, 2020
Edmonds, Washington

Written while listening to "Love Is Blindness" by U2.

**Each And Every Day**

We all have the exact same
Number of minutes
Each and every day
It all depends on how
You decide to fill them
So, choose the options
That hold permanence
And stimulate remembrance
Each and every day
To make it a well-lived life
That'll never be forgotten

November 7, 2020
Edmonds, Washington

Live life like a Lizzo song.

**The Remaining Leaves**

The remaining leaves
Steadfastly clinging
To the bare branches
Like tattered rags
Wrinkled, crinkled,
Used, and stained
Mockingly waiving
Refusing to let go

November 7, 2020
Edmonds, Washington

There's a small tree outside my office window at work that dropped 80% of its leaves in the past week. The remaining leaves are all waiving at me like, "HELLO!"

**Onward To Adventure**

Steeped in the feeling with
The recently darkened sky
Still pale around the edges
The lights newly fresh
Guiding the way
Showing where to go –
Onward to adventure
With the impending excitement
Of knowing interesting times
Are out there waiting for me
And ready to be found tonight

November 7, 2020
Edmonds, Washington

Hahaha! I'm not going anywhere! There's a pandemic going on! The song that's playing ("Roads & Lights" by Melosense) on this Spotify playlist has an album cover that shows a city street of lit-up buildings that stretch upward past the top edge of the photo, and the streetlights and more buildings continue on seemingly forever, into the twilighted night sky. The scene of that photo, along with the peppy, almost dancey, lyric-less electronic music inspired me to write this poem.

**Bonsai**

All of my life I have wanted a bonsai tree
The beauty, the small size, the patience needed
All greatly appealed to me
But, for some reason, I had never let myself get one
That changed today
Buoyed by the optimism
Created by today's election decision
Combined with the Universe putting in my path
The ideal-looking little tree
In the perfect little size
In the ideal indigo pot
Complete with little feet
And a wide-lipped rim
Featuring a big decorative rock
And two different colors
Of tiny rock chips – artfully arranged
At a booth that only sold bonsai
At the outdoor holiday market
In my town today
Where my eyes went directly to it
And stayed locked there
While I removed my wallet
And liberated the complex plant
From the booth, bringing it to my desk
Where it joys up my view
Just to the side of where I'm writing this now

November 7, 2020
Edmonds, Washington

True story.

**Dropping It All**

Dropping it all
And going
Is something I've done
Spectacularly well
Throughout this life
But each time
It gets a little harder
As I get a little older
And want to finally
Stop moving states and
Switching addresses
So I can actually
Root down in a place
Settling down
And enjoying
This life from
The current view
Which is what
I sincerely hope to do
From this moment forward

November 7, 2020
Edmonds, Washington

**The Shiny Objective**

I know what I want
But the time
Doesn't seem to be there
In the place
And the space
Where I need it
Like most things
Are lining up
But not quite right
And the misaligned corners
Are blocking
And preventing me
From moving forward
To that goal I can see
Right there
The shiny objective
Just beyond my grasp

November 14, 2020
Edmonds, Washington

**Forgotten**

The song
Epic in its length,
Breadth, and depth
Once my absolute favorite
A ten-minute masterpiece
I listened to every day
Without fail
For more than a decade
Has, somehow,
Been completely forgotten
Lying, unlistened-to
Covered with the dust
From the past fifteen years
Until today,
When I accidentally stumbled
On the memory of it
And the idea of it
Lit up my mind like a bonfire
On Spotify, seeing the album cover
Was like finding buried treasure
Pressing play, filling me solidly
With the cascading everything
That put it in my favorite position
Back when I wore youth
Like a perfectly tailored suit
Making me wonder how
And why, it had fallen
Out of favor so long ago
But thankfully it had returned
Right when I needed it the most

November 14, 2020
Edmonds, Washington

The song is “Southpaw” by Morrissey. Back in college, I named my “best of the best” cassette mixtape “Southpaw” and always found myself getting lost in the instrumental part that takes up the last half of the song.

**Favorite Thing**

For too long I've been thinking
And wanting my favorite thing
Something I only allow myself
One time a year
This time of the year
And today I went out
Bought the ingredients
Put them all together
And enjoyed it
Only to re-discover it was
Too much of a good thing
And now I'm regretting it
And remembering that every year
I've felt the same way
After indulging too much
In this favorite thing
How I want to just dump it out
(I never do)
How I try to tell myself
To never have it again
(I never do)
Because I know totally
And completely
How bad it is for me
But still
Year after year
The wanting takes hold
Making me make it
And I regret again

November 14, 2020
Edmonds, Washington

It's homemade Chex Party Mix.

**Relentless Momentum**

One
Two
Then more
Repeating
Continuing unabated
Driving steadily
Providing the foundation
Upon which the rest
Of the slowly building
Growing spectacle
Coming into view
Is traveling on
Giving the feeling
Of relentless momentum
Where, once it begins,
It will surely know no end

November 14, 2020
Edmonds, Washington

The beginning of the song "Whiteout Conditions" by The New Pornographers is what I wrote about here.

## Digging Deeply

Digging deeply
Into the ground
Is very hard
Digging deeply
Into yourself
Is impossible
To do without
Doing damage
Because of the
Buried lines
Under pressure
The live wires
Ready to shock
That might kill
If struck carelessly
All of the contents
That could come
Up to and out the top
Drowning you
With all the stuff
That once was
Buried firmly
And deeply enough
To make you think
It was forever
But you never
Counted on digging
In a shallow place
At a vulnerable time
In an area which was
Already cracked
With enough force
Which broke through
The hard-packed surface
And released everything
That was never meant
To ever be seen again

November 14, 2020
Edmonds, Washington

I wrote this while listening to “Untitled” by Interpol.

**Opinion Hosts**

On one particular network
They don’t have news anchors
Instead, they have “opinion hosts”
Those people who don’t know facts
But instead are happy to share
What they feel about daily topics
And express what the network wants
Doing no research, giving no facts –
Just their opinions in an easy, friendly
Folksy, digestible manner
Meant to be over-consumed
In unhealthy heaps, like sugar

November 14, 2020
Edmonds, Washington

**Embellishment**

A fitting end
Of the crooked establishment
Is the exaggerated embellishment
Of the crowd size today
Just like on the first day
Nearly four years ago
Which was the "biggest ever"
Despite photographic evidence
Clearly showing the opposite

November 14, 2020
Edmonds, Washington

There was the "Million MAGA March" today (one of the many names for it they could not agree on) which was only attended by a couple of thousand.

**The Past Is A Lively Cat**

The past is a lively cat
Mischievously scamping
Continuously playing
Making sleep impossible
In the middle of the night
Just following its instinct
Knocking things about
Vigorously preventing
The rest you need
From the memories
It's seeking to remind you of
While racing around,
Clumsily, at full speed

November 21, 2020
Edmonds, Washington

**A Toleration**

A toleration
Of the situation
Currently mired in
And have been
For entirely too long
At what point
Do you just give up
And give in
Out of frustration
And acceptance
That this is just how things are
Are we there yet
Or can we realize
There is another way
We can follow
That path formed by
What we most want
We can choose to leave
This stagnation we're in
And move onward
To a new place
One we never knew about
One we never planned for
The very place
Our innermost selves
Was pulling us toward
Was pushing us to
All along

November 21, 2020
Edmonds, Washington

**Early Christmas**

When things
Are so shitty
For so long
People choose
To be merry
Which is why
Everywhere you look
An early Christmas
Has taken hold
With lights, trees,
And decorations
Set up weeks early
By a tired society
Who only wants
To feel happy

November 21, 2020
Edmonds, Washington

## Standing In The Shadow

I'm standing in the shadow
Of the looming number
And I frown, wondering,
Did I set the bar too high?
Has this thing of enjoyment
Now become a burden of work?
Where I feel like I need to conform
To my own unrealistic expectations
And create content to such an extent
That I'll never be able to keep up
But the thing is
I always can
Because the well is always full
Because the ideas never stop
And my only real hardship
Is working, trying to keep up

November 21, 2020
Edmonds, Washington

**A Life Delineated By Topography**

Imagine living a life
Delineated by topography
Solely and completely
Like the kind we used to live
Hundreds of years ago
Back when we didn't have
A choice or the means
To change anything
Or to go someplace better
We just stayed in place
And dealt with the horrible hand
We were given in life
And tried to exist
In the midst of the
Merciless circumstances
We found ourselves in

November 21, 2020
Edmonds, Washington

**Smug Suits**

LinkedIn is where the smug suits
Post their definitive thoughts
On whatever business practice
They are trying to encapsulate
With the newest buzzwords,
Or people posting articles
About the company
They work for
Positioning themselves
As the authority,
Or re-posting as a way
To catch the eye of,
Or suck up to, those above
When, in actuality
They all just come off sounding
Like self-absorbed, tone-deaf,
Uncaringly conceited assholes

November 21, 2020
Edmonds, Washington

**Long Light Reaching**

Long light reaching
Over the limb of the Earth
Dawning on a new age
Or, at the very least,
A new rotation of a day
Freshly gliding into view

November 21, 2020
Edmonds, Washington

**Blizzard Of Anvils**

This started from an idea
Something I should have written months ago
But I didn't know how
And then it got buried by the months
Falling like a massive blizzard of anvils
Covering the intentions
Burying the ideas
Under the weight of responsibility
And forest fire-like current moment –
The *here* that demands attention *now*,
Not the crap that's under all of that
That's in the past, and it means nothing
Compared to the constant bullet-barrage
Pressures of the this-instant present.
The thing left behind
That idea which, at one point,
Was *so* important
Was unfortunately
Ultimately forgotten,
And completely lost to time

November 21, 2020
Edmonds, Washington

## Concepts

Concepts
Flowing
In and out
Of the mind
Like the tides
In and out
Over and over
Sometimes taking
Parts of the beach
Never to be seen again
Sometimes leaving
Something new
A fascinating thing
To occupy the mind
For part of a while
Sometimes the sky
Darkens like death
And a massive storm
Will take so much
And leave so much
Permanently changing
The landscape
Forever altering
Which isn't a bad thing
Keeping it interesting
Keeping it different
All the while
Doing the same thing
As it always has
Forever before
To forever forward

November 21, 2020
Edmonds, Washington

**Start Rowing**

When everything is new and fresh
It's beyond easy to feel so exciting
When the potential is bigger
And the desire to hop in and go
Fuels the momentum flowing
Where just merely considering
The possibilities is exhilarating
And you just can't wait
So, you jump in your boat,
Happily shove off,
And captain your way
Into a new direction

November 21, 2020
Edmonds, Washington

This is sort of an opposite answer to my "Stop Rowing" poem I wrote on December 31, 2018.

**A Commercial**

When car manufacturers create a commercial
Showing what their car can do, performance-wise
It's always the same kind of presented scenario
Of a curvaceous mountain road where their car
Is put through its paces, gripping the road
Tightly clinging to each bend and twist
While colorful leaves flit about in the wake
Of the revving and roaring engine
Braking, turning, speeding, going even faster
Working hard to keep zooming
Showing them having their way with nature

The straightaways present their own kind of fun
Being able to go all out, driving at top speed
For hours and days in a seemingly endless fashion
Where you appreciate the gentle nuanced changes
In the flat unchanging, far-stretching scenery
The kind that grabs you enthusiastically
And takes you on an unforgettable drive
Making you experience this vast country
In ways you never thought possible

Why is it always one or the other?
Why can't I readily have both?

November 21, 2020
Edmonds, Washington

**Longing For A Place**

Longing for a place
Far away
On the other side of things
Funny how it is
Back when I lived there
All I wanted
Was to be here
And now that I'm
Where I wanted to be
Hugged by the gentle hills
Of where I'm from
All I can think about
Is being back there
Seeing the snow-capped mountains
Making the tallest here
Seem like an unfunny joke
Experiencing the city
Crammed full
Of amazing things
Of surprising sites
With joyous bits of beauty
Several times a block
Every block, city-wide
And the general hopeful feeling
That seems to pervade everyday life
Where creatives lurk in every corner
Unlike here where they are celebrated
But mostly for their apparent rarity
I think I need to go
And submerge myself
In the culture of the inspired

November 21, 2020
Edmonds, Washington

November

Most of the poems I wrote tonight were fragments and partially-formed ideas that have been in my Line Ideas document for the past year or two. I dusted them off, added to them, edited, and gave them new life. I wrote most of this one about a year ago when I was living in Massachusetts and feeling the pull to move back to the Pacific Northwest.

**The Currency Of Your Life**

Your attention is everything
The seconds you have remaining
Are the currency of your life
Be sure to spend them carefully
Because soon you may not have any

November 22, 2020
Edmonds, Washington

**Early Evening On A Sunday**

The weekend that blinked by
And landed me in this place
That I really can't stand –
The early evening on a Sunday
Too late to do anything new
Other than wishing for more time
Knowing Monday morning
Will be here way too soon

November 22, 2020
Edmonds, Washington

**Shoving The Color**

There are the workers
Hurriedly erasing
All traces of autumn
With the terrible din
Of leaf blowers
Shoving the color
Pushing the crunch
Into a brusque pile
That won't last long enough
For anyone to jump in and enjoy
Before it's loaded and shredded
And hauled away to be dumped
Denying all of us the chance
To appreciate and experience
What makes the season special

November 22, 2020
Edmonds, Washington

I've never lived anywhere where the fall lasts so long. Even now, in late November, there's still some trees bursting in bright colors. But, as soon as the leaves touch the ground, landscape companies blast them into a pile and cart them away.

**Working Toward Dreams**

Working toward dreams
Or staying where it's safe
This is not a
One-or-the-other
Kind of thing
This is trying to achieve
What you most desire
Versus
The complete inaction
Of not doing anything
Declaring the latter
Means "Nice to know you,"
Because I'm moving on
To the greener pastures

November 22, 2020
Edmonds, Washington

I watched *La La Land* today, and I've been thinking a lot about this.

**At Least They Tried**

I have so much respect
For those who swung
Only to have missed
Those who broke out
And subsequently broke down
Those who left and experienced
Only to return again, defeated
Because at least they tried
They put it all out there
They reached for something
Even if they weren't successful
The respect is still with them
Because at least they tried

November 22, 2020
Edmonds, Washington

**The Danceable Happy**

The circular motion
Of the joyful melody
Joining and entwining
Filling the air
Beyond compare
With the danceable happy

November 22, 2020
Edmonds, Washington

I have *no* idea what this means. Sorry.

**Just Go Golfing**

How evil do you have to be
To be faced with the biggest
Most awful calamity ever faced
And to ignore it completely
And instead just go golfing
As if nothing was happening

November 22, 2020
Edmonds, Washington

**Autumn Is Sitting**

The autumn is sitting firmly in the place
Where the simmering summer should be
Leaving me utterly confused
As to what shenanigans this year is up to

November 22, 2020
Edmonds, Washington

This had been sitting in my Line Ideas document for a couple of months, so I finished it tonight (a little late).

**The Last Thanksgiving**

This is the last Thanksgiving
For tens of thousands
Of stubborn Americans
Who chose a tradition
Centered around dinner
Instead of protecting the health
Of family and friends
Simply by eating alone
Ensuring everyone stays safe

November 26, 2020
Edmonds, Washington

**The Deep Selfishness**

The deep selfishness
Of the proudly ignorant
Abounds and astounds
With their afflictions,
Mental and viral,
Affecting and infecting
Everyone around

November 26, 2020
Edmonds, Washington

**The Lightness Of The There**

Energy is where
It all starts –
The vibration
On the most
Universally miniscule level
With a nuance that's detectable,
Increasing,
Growing, brightening,
Affecting change
Making us feel
The remarkable difference
Between the heaviness of life
And the lightness of the There
Where we all return after here

November 26, 2020
Edmonds, Washington

## If The World Stopped Spinning

If the world stopped spinning
Would anyone notice
If we all started floating
And if they did
How would they
Deny it
Politicize it
Lie about it
Spin it in such a way
To make it a conspiracy
That's been in motion for years
Involving corrupt scientists
Who are all working in league
With long-gone politicians
In a scheme to deny their freedoms
And somehow profiting off of it

November 26, 2020
Edmonds, Washington

**A Shadow From Beyond**

A shadow from beyond
Stretching from around the corner
Originating where you can't see
Making you afraid of what exactly
Is blocking the light
And making that shape
Moving towards you
Menacingly
Making you want to leave
Quickly

November 27, 2020
Edmonds, Washington

I listened to "Not To Touch The Earth" by The Doors and wrote this creepy poem.

**The Present Is No Longer The Past**

Writing angry letters to the editor
Like they did decades ago
About how things have changed
And haven't stayed the same
Like they were decades ago
Bitter about the
Stubbornness of life
And how other people like
The things they personally don't
Which makes them so mad
That the present
Is no longer the past

November 27, 2020
Edmonds, Washington

**A Well-Dressed Seal**

Be mindful of the waters
Patrolled by orcas
Who will gladly eat you
If you venture out too far
Because, to them,
You're just a well-dressed seal

November 27, 2020
Edmonds, Washington

**Twenty Twenty**

Twenty twenty
Is the year of the hunker
Where we stayed inside
While life passed on by
Like a drive-through safari –
If you can see it from your car
Guess what? Get used to it,
That's all you can do this year
That, and watch TV
Although…
At least, you'll be able to see
Twenty twenty-one

November 27, 2020
Edmonds, Washington

**Shades Of Cloudy**

It's been weeks now
Since I've last seen
A sunset like the kind
My Instagram was comprised of
During the summer
Where painting-like scenes
Blazed across the sky
Late into the night
Each and every night
Making the brilliant spectacle
Standard fare
And the same-old thing
But with the dimming
Of the calendar for the year
We've clearly entered
The sunset-less times
Where I'm driving home
Each night in the dark
And on my days off
The sky goes from gray,
To darker gray, to black
And the world lost its joy
The brightness gone
Replaced with tones
And shades of cloudy
Making me long for the days
That stretched into weeks
Splattered with color
And filled with happiness

November 27, 2020
Edmonds, Washington

**Anchored**

Walking by a parking lot
There was a truck sitting
Close to the fence and,
In the glint of the streetlight,
I saw a single spider web
Stretching from
And connecting to
The truck and the fence
And I was impressed
With how such a tiny line
Completely anchored
And steadfastly held
Such a big thing
Firmly in place

November 29, 2020
Edmonds, Washington

## Grace

I always thought Grace
Was the unpleasant woman from accounting
From a place I worked at so long ago
But it turns out, it's a real thing, not just a person
Who turned out to be the antithesis of its meaning

November 29, 2020
Edmonds, Washington

**Perfectly Adequate**

Perfectly adequate
Could never be enough –
An offensive descriptor
Effortlessly affixed
Without consideration
Or a second of thought –
Even the blandest among us
Are brilliantly exceptional
In their own unique way

November 29, 2020
Edmonds, Washington

**The Displacement Of All Things**

This moment
Is the split second
Where time stopped
And my instinct
Is shrieking so loud
To slam on the brakes
And swing the wheel
Double-handed hard to the left
Knowing in the back of my mind
The very real potentials of
The tires squealing
The fear of crashing
The gravity threatening
The resulting tipping
The possibility of dying
The friction endured
The panic caused
The displacement of all things
In the terrible seconds
Where nothing is known
But screaming and chaos
Except for when it's over
And all of that has passed
And the forward view
Is completely new
And impossibly better
Than it could ever be before

November 29, 2020
Edmonds, Washington

Risk. Is it worth it?

# November

# DECEMBER

**Pretending The Pandemic**

Pretending the pandemic
No longer exists
Refusing to see the thousands
Who die daily
A 9/11 pile of dead
Each and every day
Fully ignoring the catastrophe
Caused by inept inaction
And constant lying
Instead choosing to focus on
How others have
Betrayed, wronged, crossed
Him
The one and only person
That truly matters
In his quickly shrinking world
Surrounded only
And completely
By mirrors

December 5, 2020
Edmonds, Washington

A quarter-million Americans get infected with the virus, and over 3,000 die, *every day*. What is the "leader" of our country doing? Playing golf non-stop and holding rallies saying how unfair everyone is to him. WTF.

**An Actual Horror Movie**

In March
We were all scared by the unknown
In May
We were all scared by the wave of deaths
In July
We felt like we might get through this
In September
We felt drained and detached from the experience
Now
Real life is like an actual horror movie
As we watch those who didn't heed the warnings
Express genuine surprise as they each
Expectedly got cut down, one-by-one
And we wonder when it's our turn
Put in actual deadly danger
By the idiots who refused to listen
And are now sleeping underground

December 5, 2020
Edmonds, Washington

**2020 Is What Happens**

2020 is what happens
When you let a little child
The cranky, bully one
Do whatever he wants
With no adult supervision
From the safety of
The crappy kids table
Diminishing our standing
Ruining our way of life
Letting the worst happen
All the while
Burning down the house
While refusing to accept
He's at fault for any of it

December 5, 2020
Edmonds, Washington

Okay, I'm done with politics and the general direness of the world for the night.

**Let's Check Her Desk**

I was sitting in a bank
Waiting for someone to help me
With something for work
When I overheard
A chorus of goodbyes
As one employee there
Was leaving for the last time
And the woman helping me
Said, "Today's her last day."
Not two minutes went by
After she left the bank
When one of her co-workers said
"She's gone. Let's check her desk"
And they went through the things
She had left behind
Like office supplies
And personal stuff
She no longer wanted
Which they divided up
While complaining
And bad-mouthing
This woman who was
Barely out of the parking lot
They all sang praises of
Just a few minutes before
Making me re-think
My company's relationship
With this financial institution

December 5, 2020
Edmonds, Washington

A true story that happened a few months ago. I was honestly shocked at how quickly all of the employees went from lavishing praise, and expressing sadness at her leaving, to talking crap about her after she left.

**I Mourn For The Autumn**

I mourn for the autumn
Whose soul lies on the ground
Cast off, strewn, and shedded
Blowing wild in the wind
Long forgotten by the arrival
Of the painful wintery chill
Forcing everyone inside
To the comfort of their TVs
Hiding unseen until the spring

December 5, 2020
Edmonds, Washington

**I Will Not Be Deterred**

I will not be deterred
From the goals I have set
My vision is unblurred
My will is concrete strong
My focus is a sniper's sight
My desire burns like the sun
All combining like Voltron
To make my dreams go from
Light and fluffy mind clouds
To an exacting perfect reality
Tangible, durable, and everlasting

December 5, 2020
Edmonds, Washington

**Freshness**

Thanks to that ex of a friend of a friend
Who I know in real-life
Who made an off-hand comment on his Instagram
Which talked about the concept and belief
That the freshness of one's creative idea
Often dictates the desired consumability of it
Which made me look at my own treasure trove of poetry
My *Line Ideas* document,
The creative treasure trove
Where I write all my ideas
Which, over the years, had grown
To over fifty-five pages.
Ideas I rarely looked at
Ideas, that when I would scroll through them,
Didn't excite me
Didn't inspire me
Didn't capture my attention enough to warrant
Saving a cutting of a phrase, or an idea
And either planting it into a fresh, blank Word document,
Or grafting it onto a stagnant line from another poem
So, I said, *screw it* and deleted all of it
Hundreds of ideas gone in a blink
More pages than most poets' chapbooks
Filled with years of their work
Was tossed into the bin and deleted
Without a smidge of remorse
All because of a post I saw on Instagram
From someone I've only met once

December 5, 2020
Edmonds, Washington

The funny thing is the bulk of this poem has been sitting in my Line Ideas document for probably two years. That night, I absolutely did delete everything I had in my previous version of

Line Ideas. I figured if I hadn't done anything with what had been fermenting for years, it probably wasn't worth saving.

Over the past week or two I've been going through Line Ideas and either using or deleting the content in it. I've trimmed it from 35 pages to 10.

Keep it fresh.

**Where Even Light Fears To Dive**

Thinking about a change
Until finding myself
Standing on the sandy edge of
Logistics too deep to consider
Dropping off quickly and impossibly
Into the wavy, inky depths
Afraid of the crushing pressure
That far into the unknown
Where even light fears to dive
Gives me the kind of pause
That resembles a complete stop
Where I spend too much time
Weighing each and every step
Well, at least the ones I can see
Numbing my toes with the wet cold
Before placing my trust completely
Into the Universe who knows
And stepping, submerging, sinking,
Someplace the me from a moment ago
Would have absolutely feared to go

December 5, 2020
Edmonds, Washington

## The Determination Of The Unstoppable

The determination of the unstoppable
The never yielding, never questioning
Never ever second guessing
Always forward-moving,
Generating the momentum
Carrying everything along
To heights and places unknown
Is the most powerful force
We could have within us

December 11, 2020
Edmonds, Washington

**The Ultimate Goal**

Poking around other Poet's websites
All the while rolling my eyes
At the pretentious types
Who would self-describe
With a capital P
As if to distinguish themselves
From the casual dabblers
And the hopeless amateurs
Despite this being a profession
Where the monetary riches
Are akin to monastery living
But still they scramble up
To get in the saddle
Of the tallest horse available
To better be loved and lauded
All the while citing a list
Of condescending publications
You may have seen them in
And spend years celebrating
Their 25-page chapbook
That someone with a pen
Once said was "groundbreaking"
Or so says the blurb on the cover
While working Submittable
Like it's a full-time job
Trying to get someone
*Anyone* to notice
To read, to *publish* their work –
The ultimate goal
Because that has worth
When added to their bio
Making it slightly longer
Making them sound
Slightly better than before

December 11, 2020
Edmonds, Washington

This week I looked up some contemporary “real” poets, the kind that make this their sole profession. I don’t know what I was expecting, but it wasn’t what I found. They all seem to write nearly nothing, but spend all of their energy solely on promoting and positioning themselves. I know that the volume of work is not indicative of quality, and it’s perfectly fine for other people to do things different than I do. However, I find it weird that some of these people are SO focused on nothing but self-promotion instead of creating. Like, there isn’t even a happy balance in there – it’s just marketing.

To me, that seems empty…soulless.

**Compared To The Me**

I was young once
And I still am now –
Not when
Compared to the me
From back then
Sporting thick hair
And innocent eyes
But I still am
Compared to the me
Fast forwarded from now
The one near the end
When, if asked
About the current me,
I would only think
Of how young
And how stupid I was
To think that 46 was old

December 11, 2020
Edmonds, Washington

**Modernly Strange**

So many friends
Now in name only
Because of Facebook
Holding us at arm's length
Giving us the knowledge
Of what they're up to
But reducing our contact
To meaningless "Likes"
And birthday reminders
Giving us just enough
To satisfy our curiosity
While making us too lazy
To be bothered with something
Like a more meaningful exchange
Which seems out of place
And modernly strange

December 11, 2020
Edmonds, Washington

**The Arco Crow**

Getting out of my car
And hearing a sound
Pulling my eyes
Across the parking lot
And up to the sign
For the gas station
Where the black bird
Noisily announced
Its repeated message
As it walked back and forth
On its elevated perch
That it is the Arco crow,
And…that's pretty much it

December 11, 2020
Edmonds, Washington

I actually tried to take a picture of the Arco crow, but it flew away before I could get my phone out of my pocket.

**The Interruption**

One moment I'm on a boat
Sloshing from side to side
Riding the intense rapids
Threatening to overturn
And toss me overboard
Several times a second
Feeling the exhilaration
And the excitement
Bringing me to new
And wonderful places
Seeing my being a tiny part
Of this energetic flow
And my mastery of it
-
When the Interruption
Stops everything entirely
Making the river instantly
Lose all of its water
And my boat thuds hard
On the muddy bottom
All forward movement
The inertia I felt
The intensity
All gone
In a jarring snap
Standing, surveying
The missing surroundings
Damning the pause
Stranding me here
Knowing the flow needed
To get me going once again
Is a sluggish process
Starting with a trickle
That can move nothing
Before it increases to a stream
Channeling around my boat
Until the depth reaches the point

Causing buoyancy and lift
Finally, movement
Painfully, lazily slow
And takes its time
Getting the depth
Getting the force behind it
Needed to push me faster
Building up to the speed
Where I start to feel
The wind again
Rushing by my face
The lifting in my spirit
As the long-dormant excitement
Begins to return
And my wits are awoken
And needed to guide me
Through the splashing
And the bouncing roughness
That's back again
As I steer my way
Through new and exciting places
Too busy
Too happy
To think of anything else but this

December 11, 2020
Edmonds, Washington

I get so deeply into the creative process when I write that this is what it's like when I get any kind of interruption that pulls me out of it, even for a moment.

**The Emerging Dawn**

The light leaks
Staining, burning
The edges of the night
As the emerging dawn
Threatens to diminish
And eventually kill
The forever darkness
The more light we see
Fuels more hope in us
Creating, fueling, driving
A self-fulfilling process
As we approach the time
When we can finally rest,
Feel safe, and actually relax
Knowing we can get through this

December 11, 2020
Edmonds, Washington

## The Lemon Is In The Way

The lemon is in the way
Assuming the manner
Often associated with
More sturdy objects
Making me pause to study
Its expressionless stance
Which is oddly strange
Because just a minute ago
It was considerably happier
When we were discussing
The lime and what it was up to
Which must mean the subject,
When reflected back at it,
Was what caused the issue
And has nothing to do with me,
Or my simple suggestion
That it give itself to my beverage

December 11, 2020
Edmonds, Washington

I like these weird ones.

I was listening to the song, "All Your Reasons" by Small Factory and saw the image for the album cover on Spotify of a crudely drawn lemon for their *I Do Not Love You* album. To me, it seemed pretty big, which inspired the first line and the title of this poem.

**Standing On A Position**

Standing on a position
Is to set a definition
Acting as a proclamation
Causing separation
Between you and them
Raising contemplation
Inspiring learning from
This perspective situation

December 11, 2020
Edmonds, Washington

I challenged myself to do a very rhyming poem.

**Just One More**

The mind whispers
"Just one more"
When you've told yourself
Absolutely no more
After this one
And when you're done
The Teletubby giggles
Squealing gleefully, "AGAIN!"
And you comply
Because, how can you not
When faced with that image
So, you exhale a sigh
And get back into it
Just once more
Seriously, that's it
You tell yourself
But you also know yourself
And what's coming next

December 11, 2020
Edmonds, Washington

**A Terrible Habit**

Constantly considering
The here-versus-there,
Always searching mindset
Or, the someplace somewhere
That's completely new
Is inherently exhausting
And is a terrible habit
That I need to refrain from

December 13, 2020
Edmonds, Washington

**Trying To Start A Train**

Working
On writing
Is like trying
To start a train
At first it seems
So impossible
Everything is so
Dense and heavy
Like it won't move
No matter how hard
You try in moving it
But somehow, budges
Ever so slightly at first
But now you can't stop
Or you'll lose momentum
So, you keep pushing hard
And the wheels are turning
Faintly, but still discernable
Just a little bit but it's enough
To keep those wheels moving
Enough so you can take a step
It's just one but it pushes you on
Before you know it, there's another
It is so hard to push this entire train
That you think you might just stop
If you do you know you'll lose
And you won't get it moving
Which makes you push harder
Trying to re-gain the momentum
Focusing on taking just another step
Because one (just one) gets you moving
In the right direction focusing on pushing
Forward, forward, always onward forward
A little faster now and it's moving even easier
The weight of the mass is lessening as it's moving
Faster goes the feet, quicker with the steps, go go go
The wind blowing on the face matches the faster pace

## December

As you realize it no longer needs your effort to roll on
And you are flat out running to try and keep up with it
So, you jump up, grab ahold, and laugh with the pure joy
At seeing what you've accomplished, getting it going like this
Rolling, going, faster than you ever could have thought possible
As you now get to relax and ride the momentum you've created
A momentum that will hopefully never need to slow or stop again

December 13, 2020
Edmonds, Washington

My second poem on this topic this month. It must be a problem for me.

**The Party Mix Of Life**

In the party mix of life
Don't be a pretzel
Or the Wheat Chex
Live like the sought-after pieces
Like a rye bread chip
Or a Corn Chex
From the bottom of the bag
Covered in flavor spices
Be the beloved best,
Not the boring bland

December 13, 2020
Edmonds, Washington

I love party mix.

**Conspiring To Dim**

Time and the turning
Of the Earth
Conspiring to dim
And extinguish
The bright neon
Blasting brightly
Across the horizon
In the brilliant finalé
Of this last-minute
Impromptu show
Diminishing the
Rusting to
Dull leather
Melting out to
Puddled twilight
Before charring
To full night

December 13, 2020
Edmonds, Washington

I can't tell you when the last time I actually saw a sunset. The first part of this has been in Line Ideas probably since the spring or the summer when I was seeing amazing sunsets every day.

**Worlds Away**

Watching a sci-fi show on TV
Where the concept of traveling
From here to somewhere that's
Worlds away with little thought
Or consideration to the distance
Or the physics involved amazes
And makes me want to know
And have that experience daily
To go worlds away just like that

December 13, 2020
Edmonds, Washington

**Running Out Of Gas**

Driving on an endless road
It's been a long while
Since I've stopped to rest
And when I look down
I'm not surprised to see
The indicator is saying
That I'm running out of gas
Because it's felt like fumes
For untold miles now
And even though
I don't know
Where I am
Part of me is okay
With letting it sputter out
Because I'm done with this
The same scenery
Passing by on repeat
Nothing new on the radio
Broken and stuck on one station
But I know it all
Forward and backward
And I've been lulled
Into getting used to
The unchanging comfort of it all
That has defined
My surroundings
For I don't know how long
But now
I'm thinking of shaking things up
Letting it run out
Coasting to a stop
Getting out
And walking
Seeing where I end up
On my own
Without my car
Without the comfort

Without knowing
What I'll be doing
Other than it'll be
Something new

December 13, 2020
Edmonds, Washington

Maybe it's the "Be Prepared"-ness that Scouting drilled into my head from a young age, but I'm really good at filling up my gas tank when it gets to a quarter left. In fact, I'm acutely aware that it's on a third of a tank right now and I should get more tomorrow. I have never in my life run out of gas, or even came close to it. What if I said, "Screw it," and let it run out? It would mess things up, but sometimes you have to shake things up like a snow globe to get you to someplace new.

**Another Squall**

Yet another squall
Striking unexpectedly
With heavy winds
Blowing me around
While I hunker down
And wait for it to pass
I wonder when can this
Consistent pattern
Of terrible storms
Actually be classified
As something more
Than just unrelated
Sporadic weather
And be declared
As the new climate
And just how
Life is now
To be endured
In this place

December 18, 2020
Edmonds, Washington

**Self-Portrait**

The self-portrait
We all paint
Of ourselves
When we meet
Someone new
Is a well-perfected
Work of art
From the repeated
Re-tellings
Re-painted
Again and again
Over the years
Slightly embellished
Expertly highlighted
Framed and placed
Skillfully on the wall
In the flattering light
Leaving the listener
Wanting to know more

December 18, 2020
Edmonds, Washington

**A New Appreciation**

A new appreciation
For positivity
And what's ideal
Is most often
Found among
The wreckage
Of terrible things
Causing pausing
Refocusing and
Redirecting
Toward reaching
That desired ideal

December 18, 2020
Edmonds, Washington

**Negligence**

Unsurprised by
The mismanagement
Causing all of this death
Still unsurprised by
The continued negligence
Delaying the vaccine
That can save everyone

December 18, 2020
Edmonds, Washington

**The War On Christmas**

This year the war on Christmas
Came from an unforeseen source
Deadly, microscopic,
And with no known
Religious affiliation
Effectively diminishing
The revered holidays
Considerably more successfully
Than any political conspiracy

December 18, 2020
Edmonds, Washington

**An Itch**

An itch is something
We never think about
It itches, we scratch it
We never consider
The reasons why
Like how maybe
An army of tiny
Microscopic critters
Are battling one another
For dominance deep down
In a crevasse in a crack
In the skin we're in
Doing so much damage
On that minuscule level
That it ripples upward
Causing their planet
To feel something –
An itch

December 18, 2020
Edmonds, Washington

**A Gloriousness Truncated**

A gloriousness truncated
Unceremoniously shortened
By those who saw fit
To ensure their own profit
At the expense of a nation
Rising with discontent

December 19, 2020
Edmonds, Washington

**The Mellow Warble**

The mellow warble
Clearly calling out
Across the meadow
From a place unseen
From a source unknown
Other than it's close by
Somewhere in the trees
And it sounds far larger
Than anything I honestly
Would ever want to meet
Making me move quickly
Inspiring my hasty retreat

December 19, 2020
Edmonds, Washington

This did not happen, but imagine if you heard an unknown animal sound that was from something that was maybe as big as a house.

**The Whisper**

The phrases
Barely spoken
In a volume
More breathy
Than wordy
The subject
Having to strain
To hear
Making out the words
From the whisper
Whose content
Is the opposite of beauty
Cutting deep
Directly through
The center
And landing
On the point
Like a knife just thrown
Stuck intensely in the heart
Still quivering slightly
Much like the subject
Hanging on each
Soundly breath
Barely uttered
But amplified greatly
Echoing, reverberating
Inside the fully-heightened shell
Needing to be filled
With whispers

December 19, 2020
Edmonds, Washington

Written while listening to "#1 Crush" by Garbage.

**Economies Of Scale**

Small, smaller, smallest
The bottom end of this
Is still gigantically huger than
What we're able to discern
With the most sensitive devices
What if it never ends
And that the further smaller
You end up going
The more it looks like
The biggest structures we know
Inside the shells of atoms
Lie entire chains of galaxies
Each filled with planets
And miniscule versions of us
Who are, in turn, even tinier
On galaxies within their atoms
In a forever looping, never-ending
Economies of scale model
That hurts the brain to contemplate

December 19, 2020
Edmonds, Washington

**Three Things That Date Us**

Looking at older
Photos and videos
The three things
That date us
Betraying the era
Decade, and year
Are fashion,
Technology,
And buildings –
Otherwise
Time would be
Hard to tell
And it would all
Blend seamlessly

December 19, 2020
Edmonds, Washington

When you are watching an older TV show and they pull out a Blackberry, or a huge brick of a flip cell phone it really pulls you out of the show.

**Instinctual**

Instinctual
Not learned
The pre-programming
That's there
From before
The beginning
The knowledge lasting
Beyond generations
That's forever
In a way that's like
Something smarter
Put it all there
To give an advantage
As a way to make sure
They could make it
Without needing
To re-learn it
Each and every time
That inside edge
Ensuring a lasting species

December 19, 2020
Edmonds, Washington

**Knock On Wood**

Knock on wood
What kind of magical properties
Does wood actually have
That plastic, Formica, or pleather
Doesn't also already carry in abundance?
What makes wood so special?
Because it was once alive
And now it's not?
Is it because we surround ourselves
With the skeletons of trees
It's like,
"I'm the lucky one,
Who's still standing
So, I'll rap on the bones
Of this chap who didn't make it."
The whole thing seems needlessly silly

December 19, 2020
Edmonds, Washington

**Sorry For The Heft**

I'm sorry for the heft
The poetic weight
Of this book you have*
That's still surprisingly light
When considering the content
I got a bit out of hand
When writing this year
And really let my creativity loose
Like a house cat
Whose never been outside before
Who discovers they're in
A rare bird sanctuary
Replace the mountains of birds
With tens of thousands of words
And you'd get me and this book

*Unless you're reading this
On an e-book reader
In which case
Please disregard my apology

December 20, 2020
Edmonds, Washington

**The Window Is Closing**

The window is closing
And the view to the goal
I have my sights on
Is quickly diminishing
Soon all I will be left with
Is a solid wall preventing
My access to the dreams
That have provided hope sustaining
Me through this time in my life
While my higher awareness
Points out that all of this time
I should have been looking
For a door so I can move forward
Rather than wasting years
Staring passively out the window

December 20, 2020
Edmonds, Washington

**To Be Excluded**

I know it's completely true
That each rejection received
Is a note from the Universe
Saying, "That wasn't for you,"
But it still hurts to be excluded
which feels so much worse

December 20, 2020
Edmonds, Washington

Six months ago I submitted the first portion of this poetry collection to be considered for a poetry award, which included getting published by their small press. Back in the summer, I sent in my poems to a bunch of different things, which is something I normally don't do. This afternoon, I got the rejection…which I will say it was a *great* rejection, but it was still a rejection.

I'm going to stop sending in my work to places. Back in the summer, I felt like "getting published" was the only path to advancing my work because it seems like all of the well-known and talked-about poets do this. I am not competing with them, or anyone. I write for one person – me. If others happen to discover it and enjoy it, great, that's awesome, but I'm not going to become singularly-focused on submitting 24/7.

I need to create, so I will spend my time creating.

**Walking Trees**

Everything changes
Nothing ever stays the same
So be prepared
For everything to be different
And be flexible like the trees
Who bend to ride out the wind
Well, maybe that might not be
The most descriptive analogy
Because trees can't move around
Let me re-phrase that a bit…
Be flexible like walking trees
Who bend to ride out the wind,
Move to avoid crashing cars,
And walk to be in better places
Because that's the best way to be

December 20, 2020
Edmonds, Washington

I had no idea I would end up there when I started writing this.

## The Darkest Day

Tomorrow is the darkest day
When the sun doesn't wake up
Until after eight in the morning
And it goes to bed all too early
At four in the afternoon
But after that, things change
And, day by day
It gets brighter earlier
And stays day even later
Sliding us along
Through the winter months
Into the warm embrace of spring

December 20, 2020
Edmonds, Washington

**Removing The Ritual**

It was something special
An evening planned
Reviews read
A movie selected
A time chosen
Get dressed, go out,
Go to the theater
Filled with anticipation
Get tickets
Buy too-expensive snacks
Get tickets ripped
Choose seats
Watch dumb commercials
Get excited as the lights dimmed
Sit through twenty minutes of previews
Get excited again when the movie started
Watch the movie
Singularly focused on this one thing
Feeling the excitement and reaction
From everyone in the theater
Until it's over when you gather up and go
Walking out with a theater full of others
Who shared the same experience as you
And then the drive home
Discussing what you just saw
And I personally added the additional step
Of logging this viewing in a spreadsheet
Along with all of the other movies I've seen
In a theater for the past few years
But now
In 2020
Everything's changed
The movies are delayed
The theaters have closed
And the specialness
Of the experience
Has been left behind

Unceremoniously replaced
Streaming movies
On our home TVs
Surrounded by distractions
Pets, phones, normal life
The very thing we used to deliberately mute
For two whole hours when we saw a movie out
Removing the ritual
The very thing that made it something more
Leaving us poorer than the year before
Adding another thing
To the very long list
That 2020 has taken from us

December 25, 2020
Edmonds, Washington

Today, I saw *Wonder Woman 1984* on HBO Max. I was disappointed in the movie that I had been so patiently and excitedly waiting for, but I also did not like the removal of the whole movie-going experience. Seeing movies in the theater has always been something I *really* loved to do, and I'm afraid that this is the future of movies – that they won't be the big huge productions that they are now, and that they'll just be made for TV, completely removing the theater experience.

**Conjunction**

It all depends on the perspective
From out there it seems like
Nothing at all is happening or different
From here, they seem to be
Magnetically attracted
As we watched with increased fascination
Seeing them get closer and closer
Approaching one another
Over several months
Anticipation building
Seeing them grow closer
Destined to reach out
And almost touch
In the conjunction
Completely unviewable
From my location
Due to a rainy stretch

December 25, 2020
Edmonds, Washington

Jupiter and Saturn. Thankfully, I did end up seeing them a few days after the conjunction when they were still very close.

**Expanding Throughout**

Sitting, meditating,
Silencing, quieting,
Feeling the building
Reaching out
Lifting up
Expanding throughout
Being everything
Being everywhere
Bathed in ethereal light
Experiencing energy
Living a lightness
Beyond we can see

December 25, 2020
Edmonds, Washington

Wow, I love meditating.

**The Flicker Of Flame**

The flicker of flame
The living, dancing light
A fleeting existence
Repeating instantly
Consuming its fuel
Warming and entrancing
Setting the soothing scene
For those enjoying it carefully
Or, lasting in its permanence
In the memories of those
Touched by it angrily –
Fire is an interesting thing
Affecting people differently
Depending on their experience

December 25, 2020
Edmonds, Washington

**Erode The Rust**

Shifting thought
Enough to ensure
Changed belief
Is like moving
Something heavy
At first it seems
It's impossible
But when you try
Is when you find
That it can move
Just a little at first
But that's enough
To erode the rust
Formed on your
Firmed principles
Making it easier
For future change
To work its way
Into your mind

December 27, 2020
Edmonds, Washington

**Poolside**

Soft and easy
By the poolside
Feeling the warmth
Radiating downward
On your bare skin
Recently wrinkled
By a leisurely lap
In the sparsely populated pool
Made so by the odd time
Chosen to ensure this moment
Would happen just like this

December 27, 2020
Edmonds, Washington

Listening to Poolside's cover of "Harvest Moon." I like the very chill feeling this song has, and it made me think of someone relaxing by a pool in the summer.

It's a nice contrast to my cold hands that I have to keep warming between typing on the keyboard.

**To Be A Movie Star**

It must be nice to be a movie star
And, decades later, see your film
And the younger version of yourself
Perfectly preserved for all of forever
With styled hair, special wardrobe,
Idealized lighting, and the team of people
Whose only job is to make you look
Your absolute best for the camera
Always updated to the newest format
So it can always be seen by everyone
While the rest of us only have
Rare faded photographs
Poorly posed, red-eyed,
Squinting at the flash
In photo albums never seen
Because they're not in a phone

December 27, 2020
Edmonds, Washington

**The Hatred Espoused**

They think it's okay
Because others are expressing it
Embolden by the tweets
From the very top
Seeing the flags
Flying from trucks
Viewing the actions
Recorded by others
Hearing only the echoes
They've chosen to place around,
Surrounding themselves
With the same thoughts
The hatred espoused
Over and over again, until
It is so deeply engrained
That they think it's okay
To publicly express
Repulsive things
To demean others
At the grocery store
To say the stuff
That is not acceptable
That has no place
In any society
And when they do
The spotlight shines
Directly on them
Bringing to light
Their detestable actions
Making employers fire
Making their friends ignore
Making spouses leave
Making them
The vile pariahs
Cast out and alone
And kept there
Forever more

With Google searches
Showing their true nature
And what they're capable of

December 27, 2020
Edmonds, Washington

I saw two news articles in the past day about this. One was a nurse who recorded herself flashing a "white power" hand signal, the other was a police officer who had a secret account where he advocated the killing of judges and officials who had political views he disagreed with. Both were, thankfully, fired.

In cases like this, I always think of them years from now, applying for a job, or meeting new people, who end up Googling them, seeing what they did, and abruptly having nothing to do with them.

**A Cute Fuzzybutt**

The surprisingly fast
Jumping hopping
Of a cute fuzzybutt
Scamping around
Playfully scurrying
All the while singing
Constantly meowing
Meowing meowing
Amid the batting
And scattering
Of everything
In her pawed path

December 27, 2020
Edmonds, Washington

Bunny the cat has three legs (missing her left-front leg), and she normally walks slowly…except when she's in a hurry – then she can move surprisingly fast in her playful, hopping way.

**The Bulking Time Of The Year**

Looking at the calendar
Seeing we're right in
The bulking time of the year
From Thanksgiving
Through New Year's
And for a while afterward
Because eating better
Doesn't turn on a dime
Or change in a day
For that matter
So, we give in
And vow to change
Sometime next year

December 27, 2020
Edmonds, Washington

Why yes, I *am* having a cheese log and Triscuits for dinner. It's okay because we're between Christmas and New Year's.

**A Landscape Changed**

This year has produced
A landscape changed
So completely and severely
That not even the most dystopian
Of science fiction authors
Could have ever foreseen
The chaos unleased
On a world so unprepared
For anything remotely like this
I am so beyond thankful
That me and mine
Made it through 2020
Relatively unscathed
Apart from being bruised
(Which was to be expected)
Considering the alternative
That is okay and greatly favored
As far as outcomes go

December 27, 2020
Edmonds, Washington

**A Much-Deserved Break**

So glad it's over
But I'm still afraid
As bad things
Don't magically stop
Just because the calendar
Decided to flip
From one year to another
That it could continue,
Multiply, and magnify
As it's done all year
Still though, we can have hope
It might actually
Work out in our favor
Without having anything
To base it on
Other than we need
A much-deserved break
Which has got to be something
That has some weight
With whatever in the Universe
Makes these kind of decisions

December 31, 2020
Edmonds, Washington

Happy New Year!

December

## IF YOU ENJOYED THIS COLLECTION

Please consider rating it at Amazon.com. As an independent author, having people review my works is critical in helping to increase my exposure and letting new people discover books like this. Thank you!

**WRITTEN BY ERIC NIXON**

***The Year That Aged Us*** – 2020 poetry collection
***You Are A Poet*** – guided poetry journal
***Caught In Pause*** – 2019 poetry collection
***Equidistant*** – 2018 poetry collection
***The Cupcake*** – 2017 poetry collection
***2492: Attack Of The Ancient Cyborg*** – science fiction novel
***The Ocean Above*** – 2016 poetry collection
***Cascadia's Fault*** – 2015 poetry collection
***The Taborist*** – 2014 poetry collection
***The Entire Universe*** – 2013 poetry collection
***Trying Not To Blink*** – 2012 poetry collection
***Lost In Thought*** – poetry collection
***Emily Dickinson – Superhero: Vol. 1*** – historical fiction novel
***Incident On The Hennepin*** – a short story set in *2492*
***Plenty Of Time*** – short story
***Retribution On A Jetpack*** – a short story set in *2492*
***Anything But Dreams*** – poetry collection

Available at Amazon.com/author/ericnixon

## ABOUT THE AUTHOR

Eric Nixon is the poet and author of eleven poetry collections, a guided poetry journal, several short stories, and two novels – *2492: Attack Of The Ancient Cyborg*, and *Emily Dickinson, Superhero: Vol. 1*. His poetry has been featured on *The Writer's Almanac*. Eric lives in Edmonds, Washington with his author wife, Kari Chapin.

www.ingramcontent.com/pod-product-compliance
Lightning Source LLC
Chambersburg PA
CBHW020845090426
42736CB00008B/244

* 9 7 8 0 9 9 8 4 3 6 2 6 5 *